The Strategic SENCo

The Strategic SENCo

How to lead whole school inclusion with vision and purpose

Kenny Wheeler

BLOOMSBURY EDUCATION

LONDON   OXFORD   NEW YORK   NEW DELHI   SYDNEY

BLOOMSBURY EDUCATION
Bloomsbury Publishing Plc
50 Bedford Square, London WC1B 3DP, UK
Bloomsbury Publishing Ireland Limited
29 Earlsfort Terrace, Dublin 2, D02 AY28, Ireland

BLOOMSBURY, BLOOMSBURY EDUCATION and the Diana logo are trademarks of
Bloomsbury Publishing Plc

First published in Great Britain 2025 by Bloomsbury Publishing Plc

This edition published in Great Britain 2025 by Bloomsbury Publishing Plc

A catalogue record for this book is available from the British Library

ISBN: PB: 978-1-80199-681-5; ePub: 978-1-80199-683-9

2 4 6 8 10 9 7 5 3 1 (paperback)

Typeset by Newgen KnowledgeWorks Pvt. Ltd., Chennai, India
Printed and bound in Great Britain by TJ Books, Padstow, Cornwall

MIX
Paper | Supporting
responsible forestry
FSC
www.fsc.org   FSC® C013056

To find out more about our authors and books visit www.bloomsbury.com
and sign up for our newsletters

For product safety related questions contact productsafety@bloomsbury.com

Contents

1 Let's start with a vision…

Whether you are a new SENCo or an experienced, long-serving SENCo, it is really important for you and the people you work alongside and those you lead to understand what all your efforts and hard work are going to contribute towards and achieve in the longer term. Working in the world of SEND can be all-consuming, with a scarcity of resources, staff and time. There is no doubt you are going to be busy, and that you will be drawn and pulled in several directions, so you need to be clear about the direction you are heading in, rather than just operating in the here and now. There is a risk that we get stuck into the work we feel is the most urgent and important, or which others present as the most urgent and important, but we need to have absolute clarity about what we are doing and how it will lead to long-term strategic change.

Spending time thinking about the longer term helps us come up with a vision that will inspire and motivate people to want to do well and fully commit to our cause. This vision needs to be about the greater good and show that through the culmination of all our efforts we can make a real positive difference to the most vulnerable learners in our setting. The clear vision also provides us with an anchor which we can constantly refer back to when considering what work we need to undertake. If what we are doing or being asked to do is not going to progress us towards our vision, then we can quite rightly say no. We can push back on having more layers or work added to our systems when they aren't going to add value to what we are doing, and may in some cases distract us from our overall vision.

Invest the time in coming up with a clear, meaningful vision that you and your team believe in passionately and you will have a powerful tool to drive change in the long term. You will have something to refer back to when you are asked: 'Why are we doing this?'. Quite simply your response will refer back to your vision, linking in the 'why' behind what you are asking others to do. This is a great opportunity to create a 'We, Us, Together' culture; it is not about individuals, it is about your team making a positive difference through collaboration and commitment. Together, we can achieve great things for the benefit of all learners but especially for those who struggle to engage or access the curriculum and often the wider learning environment.

Changing the status quo

Another consideration is that we may encounter a situation in which people think that the SEND provision and practices are OK so why change things? 'We've always done it like this!' is an oft-heard statement. This doesn't make it right nor does it mean we have to settle for someone else's standards or systems that were put in place some time ago!

We know the profile and needs of learners is different to what they were a decade ago. We also have the (what seems to be enduring) issue of the legacy from Covid-19 and lockdown during which learners may not have interacted so much socially, may have experienced trauma or may not have engaged fully with learning, so we are dealing with different needs. Different needs, different issues accessing the curriculum and different characteristics requires different thinking, so we have to have some clarity around what we are actually going to do differently.

Resources are scarcer and staff cutbacks have happened, so in some respects we are being challenged to do more with less. Recruitment is also challenging, meaning that even if we do have funding for new staff, finding them is becoming increasingly challenging. Part of our different approach needs to start with thinking about the classroom environment. Rather than have an additional provision- and intervention-led approach we need to consider what happens in the classroom in the first instance. If we get it right in the classroom then there is going to be less need for catch-up and keep-up, boosters. Our different approach therefore needs to be more creative but draw on the resources we do have, which are: great teachers, great teaching assistants, great school staff full stop. We need to think about what we can do differently to better meet the needs of a more complex cohort of learners.

Every year we get data informing us that outcomes for learners with SEND are not as positive as those for learners without SEND. What we are doing doesn't seem to be making a difference. If we continue what we are currently doing, then we are surely going to continue the cycle where learners are simply not suitably prepared or ready for the next stage of education, training or employment. This can't continue to be a tragic and damning indictment on the current education system: we need a new vision, new behaviours, new thinking and different practices leading to different outcomes.

That cursed hamster wheel

It is easy to get drawn into the annual school cycle, in which year on year the same activities and events play out just like clockwork. Even though they happen every year, it feels as if we still sometimes get caught out by events and are surprised when they come round again. Our efforts are very much focused on maintaining operational aspects of the role. It is in no way a criticism if this is the situation you find yourself in, but what is going to change if you are working like this from week to week and term to term? It is at this point we need to allow ourselves time to think about the longer-term goal(s) we are hoping to achieve. This then brings us back to the importance of having a vision to drive longer-term, more strategic thinking and actions.

We need to give ourselves permission to stop what we are doing and think about the longer term strategic goals we want to achieve. If we don't give ourselves permission, then we are condemning ourselves to the same discussions year on year. The same hard slog before public assessments where we bolster performance but exhaust ourselves and our staff with layer upon layer of interventions and additional support. In many cases we don't even know the scale of difference some of the additional support is making because we either feel or are told it just needs to be put in place. How do we objectively measure the difference our exam boosters are having on our learners?

It is the curse of the hamster wheel: we get on it in September, blink and realise it is July! This is all the more reason to give ourselves permission to get off the wheel and consider our strategic intent. It also gives us the opportunity to take stock of what is happening across the academic year and identify when strategic actions need to take place. Essentially, across the weeks or months, we need to commit to focusing on the strategic so that longer term changes do take place and are not just pipe dreams.

One of the reflections we need to have when we go to work is whether we are going to lead purposefully or whether we are going to sleepwalk. Leading purposefully means we go in with intent, it means we are going to do something that will effect change in our setting. Sleepwalking happens, we all do it, but what it means is we aren't leading change. And if we aren't leading with purpose or intent, then what are all those staff in our team going to do?

We know the urgent and important tasks are always going to be there but that shouldn't be an excuse for accepting that it is OK to be working in this way. We have the power to change what is happening, we can influence how we and others operate in our setting. We just need to give ourselves some time to stop and think about what it is in the long term we are trying to achieve. Do we want to be known for our dedication to responding to emails or do we want to be known for influencing inclusive practices across our setting? If we can't articulate our vision, then how do we expect others to understand the rationale behind why we are asking them to undertake particular tasks or roles?

Clarity of vision

What is your vision for SEND? It is worth taking a step back and thinking about what you want SEND and whole school practices to look like in your setting. Yes, there may be a plethora of challenges we as SENCos currently face but how do we want things to look in the future? We need to explore the 'Why' behind what we are setting out to achieve and support our team and colleagues to consider what all the effort and hard work is going to lead to. This is a good opportunity to consider the moral purpose behind the work we and others are going to undertake over the course of an academic year and beyond. Through our small steps, we need to consider what our destination is in the longer term. This is not a naïve, overly optimistic exercise but one that declares our intent and high expectations we have for our school community. It is not just about achieving more for our learners but empowering staff, including stakeholders, and developing a more inclusive school setting.

Imagine being a staff member sitting in a meeting and you have a leader in front of you talking about everything you are going to do over an academic year, but they can't actually explain the purpose behind it all. That is going to be pretty frustrating. After all, there has got to be more to what we are doing than just hard work. There has to be an ultimate goal that will lead to a better future. If we have clarity about what we are working towards and the greater good it will do, then we won't just get people doing their job, we will make them passionate and engaged so they go the extra mile – because they understand how what they do makes a difference. We aren't just turning up and working with learners, we are shaping the future and giving learners a better chance in life.

It really is important that you have clarity behind what you are doing because that vision acts as an anchor. That vision makes the difference between saying yes or no to what may seem like competing priorities. It gives you a point to build justification behind changes and different approaches. It can stop staff going off on tangents because you have given them a clear direction which steers their work. Ultimately, it can help harness our collective efforts so we are not just working hard but more importantly we are working *effectively*, towards the same compelling vision and goals. It can also help ensure that you have the right people on your team, people who share your passion, commitment and determination to achieve a better future.

Thinking time

So, let's take some time to think about what it is you want to achieve with SEND in your setting. I don't think it really matters if you are an outstanding school or one in contrasting circumstances. However, I do think it is important to be clear about your intent for your most vulnerable learners, if not just for yourself, then for colleagues and the wider community (learners, parents, governors). What is it you are going to do to develop a clear sense of belonging in your setting and get commitment and support from all your stakeholders?

It might be helpful to be messy at this point and just jot down all the things you would like to achieve in the long term. I find it helpful to visualise what a better future will look like and involve. When I am walking around a school, what will I see, what will I hear and what will I feel? Rather than just being emotive or ephemeral we might also have some data references e.g. a reduction in NEET, suspensions or exclusions, or improved attendance and engagement in wider school life. All data points for better outcomes, through our high expectations and commitment to ensure a better future for all.

Outline what positive practices will be taking place and what learners will be able to do and achieve as a result of inclusive practices at the school. This might also include what relationships with various stakeholders will look like, e.g. parental engagement is positive with good attendance at various workshops or parent consultation meetings. It might be that instead of expecting parents to come to the school we meet in a neutral setting which leads to better engagement.

You might even want to draw what your ideal SEND future at the school looks like. What will you see different groups doing in the future? You can sketch out different groups with the various activities they might be engaged in along with the emotions they are feeling at the time. It is absolutely fine to be messy and have lots written down because this is the starting point. From this point we can edit down what we have so that we end up with a couple of sentences, a paragraph or a visual for what we want to achieve. If you opt for the visual option it might still be worth having a few sentences which will help you succinctly describe what is going on and why it is so important to achieve.

Examples of your SEND vision might include something like having all learners in classrooms with teachers being able to adapt their approaches in order to engage individuals so they can better access the curriculum. It might also be less utilitarian and could focus on learners accessing the wider school curriculum and participating in activities alongside their peers. It could be the whole community coming together, working in unison to support a better future for all.

Whatever you end up with, your vision needs to be compelling because this will influence whether people want to work towards it or not. The strength of your vision and how you articulate it will influence who wants to join you on your journey. This is not just about doing your jobs; it is about the commitment and dedication you demonstrate through your eternal optimism that things will be better in the future. This is a declaration of your leadership; people will want to do things for you not because they have to or feel they should but because they fully believe that what you are doing is inherently the right thing to do.

Sharing your messy vision

SEND and inclusion are not the sole responsibility of the SENCo, so you need to take your messy first draft and edited versions and talk them through with a trusted colleague. It might be worth exploring what they see as the most important things for learners to work towards or for staff to realise what their efforts are trying to achieve. This stage is important because you cannot be the only person in your setting holding the SEND megaphone to champion inclusion. We need to create a compelling vision so that others are willing and committed to sharing the megaphone so SEND and inclusion are on the agenda across the school. It is also worth checking how your vision links in with that of the whole school. Is there common language or is some editing necessary so that there is alignment?

The challenge here could be if your vision does not align with the school vision. This might necessitate discussions with senior leaders and governors to explore how both can be revised to give clear, up-to-date visions for the whole school and for the SEND/Inclusion team. What can we do as a group of professionals to ensure that every learner in our setting has the best possible educational experience? If there are groups who are not receiving that, then maybe we do need to re-think our whole school vision, so we have lived values and not laminated ones! Does every learner who attends the school believe that they can do well and does every member of staff believe that they can succeed?

So, involve others, listen, understand their views and consider what you might need to do to edit your vision so you will get buy-in from colleagues and support from wider stakeholders. As you refine your vision it will become clearer in your head; you should also feel more comfortable articulating it as it is refined and revised. Short and to the point is fine and probably essential.

You don't want to be reciting *War and Peace* in front of colleagues because they are likely to switch off. In a succinct way, what are we aiming for?

Vision and leadership

In terms of leadership, having a vision is essential. If we can articulate what we are working towards, then we can help others understand what it is we are trying to achieve. This is not a one- or two-year goal or target but something we will work towards over time, and in doing so we will make experiences better for all in our setting. It can also outline the moral purpose behind what we want to achieve. We have to change the narrative around SEND and inclusion so we avoid the miserable annual datasets telling us yet again that outcomes are not good enough and we have yet again failed numerous learners who needed us to have done something differently. So, what is it we are going to do in order to make sure that all our learners are prepared for their next stage of education, employment or training?

The other reason why having a vision is important because we can use it for several purposes, such as meetings, training or to set targets, all of which will help us when leading SEND and inclusion.

Avoiding shiny objects

There are numerous initiatives in SEND: lots of projects to get involved with and lots of new interventions to roll out in your setting, all of which seem really great. The problem is, we already know we are busy and that any new commitment is going to impact on what we are already doing. The litmus test therefore is 'how does this new project, initiative or intervention link in with our vision?'. If there is no strong link to our vision, then as much as we might want to undertake the project or roll out the intervention, the answer simply has to be no. Part of the leadership side of being a SENCo is feeling comfortable saying no. Ultimately, there is an opportunity cost: if we are saying yes to X, what are we saying no to?

Linking work with our 'why'

Equally, it is helpful to use the vision when you are contemplating asking others to undertake tasks. Is what you are asking others to do going to help in making progress towards the vision? It may be that you need to consider your systems or processes so that colleagues and other stakeholders can clearly see the purpose behind what you are asking them to do or are proposing that they do. In SEND there is sometimes the pressure to undertake tasks or activities because that is what we have been led to believe needs to be done. Interactions and conversations with SENCo colleagues can sometimes leave us feeling that we should be doing more because that is what others seem to be doing in their settings. Shining a light on practices, asking why we are doing something and how it will help us in the longer term can help remove unnecessary tasks. Bring it back to your vision: how will completing the task or activity help us in making progress towards your longer-term vision? Don't feel guilty about saying no or removing an activity which has previously been used if it doesn't align with the vision. Doing that doesn't mean you are changing things just for the sake of it, it just means you are focused on doing a few things well. From experience, don't feel guilty saying no and don't respond if someone accuses you of not being a team player.

Making clear our moral purpose

The other benefit of having a clear vision which is communicated across your team and setting is that it gives purpose to what you are doing or asking others to do. An example of this might be when you are in a staff meeting and are outlining what you want staff to do as part of whole school approaches to SEND. It is only natural for staff to perhaps question why they are being asked to undertake specific tasks when they have so much to do already. You can use your SEND vision to remind staff what it is you are striving for and how what you are asking will help make progress towards the vision. It may also be the case that you are asking staff to do X instead of Y so it is important to make clear that some work is not an extra layer but an alternative one.

Recruiting the right people and allowing others to leave

The vision also extends to future recruitment. Anyone who applies to work in your team needs to know what the vision is and needs to be committed to supporting the ongoing work to realise it. You can also explore how the individual's skills and qualities will help and how their values align with the vision.

This can then help ensure you can build a team who are fully onboard and committed to supporting the team and colleagues in making progress.

Conversely, it may also mean that some staff feel that they do not align with how the team is progressing and that they will be better placed to work elsewhere. Whilst this is sad in some ways, it is better to have half a committed team than a full team who contradict and work against long-term goals. Having staff leave is not necessarily a bad reflection on your leadership. It may just be the case that the job they were doing is not going to be the same, so they want to move on because it is no longer for them. Your clear, passionate vision can help in recruiting replacements over time, individuals who are committed to the cause.

Highlighting positive urgency rather than just negative urgency

For decades we have been talking about the poor outcomes for learners with SEND. We have had government officials and national experts share worrying statistics about what happens in later life to individuals who have special educational needs. We have changed legislation, the curriculum, the Code of Practice and things aren't getting any better. It is not to say we don't share the harsh reality if we don't get better at supporting individuals and preparing them for adulthood. What we do need to do is share the positive urgency.

We need to focus on the positive urgency of engaging with more inclusive practices. We have to highlight the benefits to learners, families, colleagues and a wider range of stakeholders. If your stakeholders get onboard and join you on your journey you need to highlight what benefits they will see. For instance, high quality adaptive teaching could result in less time spent developing individual resources. Clearer scaffolding could enable more learners to access lessons as they feel better able to engage with content. It could even be the case that off task behaviour is reduced as more learners feel they can access and understand what they need to do. Take some time to think about the positives that will arise if others get onboard and support your vision.

Why would people follow you?

Finally, consider the vision as an advert for you as a leader. This is an opportunity for you to communicate your passion, commitment and dedication to improving inclusive practices for all learners. The vision is a way for you to get more than people just doing their jobs. The right vision brings wholehearted commitment and engagement. Think about the difference between management and leadership. People do things for *managers* mainly because of the hierarchical aspect: you do something because your boss has asked you to. People do things for *leaders* because they believe in them. This is not a case of compliance; you are appealing to the intrinsic drive and motivation individuals have. They are going to do something because it is going to help all of you make progress on the fantastic journey towards your vision, which they believe in!

Reflection time

Take some time here to jot down a couple of sentences describing what you feel your vision is. Remember, this doesn't need to be perfect, but it does need to happen - you need to have something to edit, adjust and refine. It should however give you a sense of pride and a warm feeling inside that makes you think "Yes! This is what I want to work towards".

_____
_____
_____
_____
_____
_____
_____

How does that feel? Does the statement encapsulate what you want to achieve in the long run? Leave it for a little while and then have another go at editing and refining your vision below:

_____
_____
_____
_____
_____
_____
_____

What feedback are you getting from colleagues you have shared your messy vision with? What further adjustments do you think you need to make?

_____
_____
_____
_____
_____
_____
_____

How does your vision align with that of your school? Is there anything you need to adjust before you share it with leaders?

_____
_____
_____
_____
_____
_____
_____

What is your positive urgency? What positive message will you share to encourage colleagues and wider stakeholders to engage with your plans?

_____
_____
_____
_____
_____
_____
_____

2 Knowing your context

Every school is unique

We know that every school is unique but what is it about your setting that makes it different from all the other schools across the country? This is a really important starting point to establish. It's also worth thinking about how it has changed over time. The danger is that in a busy world we continue doing what has always been done – but do these approaches match what is needed by the current and future cohort?

Whole school data

Starting with the whole school data, you might be able to identify particular characteristics that set your school apart from national or regional trends. It could be that there is a gender imbalance or that the school has high mobility or low levels of pupil premium.

Other data we receive can also give us key insights into the cohorts we receive as a school. For instance, how many learners achieve a good level of development at Reception? How many learners did not pass the phonics screening? What were overall writing levels for Key Stage 2 SATs? All this data provides an insight into the nature of learners we are working with on a day-to-day basis. It can also reveal where learners may be experiencing some level of difficulty.

All the data we have at our disposal will tell us a story about our schools. So, what is the story behind your own school? What does that mean in terms of how you go about supporting your learners?

SEND Identification

Before we go any further with context it would be good to broach the issue of SEND identification in settings. We know from research into primary settings that the biggest factor influencing whether a learner is identified as having special educational needs is down to the school they attend (Educational Policy Institute, Identifying pupils with special educational needs and disabilities, March 21). Essentially, a child could be identified as having special educational needs in one setting but would not in another. So just how confident are we in our identification of SEND across our settings?

We often talk about the post code lottery impacting on the support schools are able to access. However, it appears the case that there is a lottery as to whether learners are identified as having special educational needs or not. There are 317 local authorities across the whole of England, each of them likely to have their own approach to supporting schools with SEND. So there are many varying messages being communicated to schools as to identifying learners who may have special educational needs. Also add in multi-academy trusts who might advocate their own approach, and we have a plethora of different messages circulating across the system.

How do we identify SEND?

The Code of Practice, Chapter 6.15 states that:

> *A pupil has SEN where their learning difficulty or disability calls for special educational provision, namely provision different from or additional to that normally available to pupils of the same age.*

Now whilst this seems on the surface to be a pretty straightforward statement, there are quite a few things that impact on identification of SEND in different settings. The main point that varies from context to context is what constitutes 'different from or additional to' provision. We also need to consider the Equality Act 2010 and think about whether provision is merely a reasonable adjustment or whether it is indeed 'different from or additional to' that which other learners receive.

In some settings and across some Local Authorities, there has been the introduction of Ordinarily Available Provision. This is effectively what the local authority expects the core offer to be from every school. It outlines what the local authority feels every learner should be entitled to so they can access the curriculum and wider learning environment. The reflection for you as a SENCo is wondering how the Ordinarily Available Provision (OAP) is adopted by staff and is used to inform classroom practices. We will look at this again in the chapter on high-quality teaching.

Booster, catch-up or special educational need?

Just to add a few other considerations into the mix, it is worth reflecting on the difference between a learner needing some support to get them back on track and them needing sustained provision over time. There will be times when some learners require additional provision; however, if this helps them catch up or better access the curriculum or wider learning environment then perhaps they don't need to be identified as having special educational needs. It doesn't mean they can't go on a monitoring list to check how they are progressing over time, but they might not need to be identified as having SEND.

If we place a learner on a booster or catch-up and it doesn't have the impact we had hoped, then we need to consider our next steps. If a structured intervention has not made a difference, then we need to consider the possibility that the learner may have a special educational need. Using the graduated approach, we can apply our assessment of the individual and then work out what would be the next most appropriate type of provision to help target their needs. It is likely at this point that we would place the learner on the school's SEN list with a clear understanding of when progress, support and additional provision will be reviewed.

Does a diagnosis automatically mean SEND?

The other consideration when deciding to place a learner on the school's SEN list links to when an individual has a formal diagnosis. There is some heated debate around this topic with strong views in both camps. Some feel that a diagnosis should automatically mean a learner is placed on the school's SEN list because they have a recognised disability. Others feel that the Equality Act and Code of Practice should be considered as some support for an individual may well constitute a reasonable adjustment and therefore is not 'different from or additional to' provision. Essentially, you can adjust practices, approaches or supply resources that will help the individual to access the curriculum and wider learning environment without them needing any further targeted or specialist provision.

It comes down to the decisions made at a school level and could perhaps be a reflection of how inclusive a setting is. Some schools may consider additional targets for a learner and additional strategies for teachers as additional provision, whereas other settings may just see this as good practice and part of their core offer. Equally, if all you are doing is sharing targets with no other provision being put in place, then is this really additional provision?

Whilst a diagnosis can be helpful in identifying possible support strategies and accessing additional support, it does not always tell us much about the individual. The diagnosis may well tell us about a difficulty, disorder or disability but it might not give us a detailed picture of the individual. Part of the challenge is understanding the individual, what might inhibit or impact on them accessing the curriculum, which teaching strategies might work and which strategies they themselves may adopt to help. The diagnosis helps add information which we can add to the jigsaw in better understanding an individual, but the diagnosis is in itself not the whole jigsaw.

Ultimately, the diagnosis debate comes down to needing to have conversations with learners and their families. Consider the following three aspects.

- What support would be most appropriate for an individual?
- How can this be met through your ordinarily available provision and reasonable adjustments?
- What additional provision may be necessary?

Part of this also needs to focus on the steps to help the learner prepare for their next steps in education. Any additional provision needs to help develop independence not dependency.

- What does each party need to do in order to best prepare the learner for the future challenges they will face?

What does our data tell us?

We have at our disposal a wealth of data that will not just give us an overview of learners with SEND but provide information at a more granular level. We have the ability to drill down and understand the key characteristics of learners with SEND across our setting, rather than seeing them as one homogenous group.

The importance of analysing our school population data is key to helping us reflect on what we actually know about the learners we are supporting. Quite simply, are we working on data or judgements? Is data driving key decision-making or are our personal judgements (and those of others) influencing how we develop inclusive practices? Let's be clear, there is nothing wrong with using our professional judgements, but do they consider the holistic picture? Equally, could they be affected by personal agendas, egos or bias?

When we draw on the data, we can break it down to give us more insight behind the learners we are looking to support. The 'drilling down' gives us a little more context to start questioning possible underlying reasons behind the need for a pupil to receive additional provision and support.

Breaking the data down in one place

Schools have their own approaches and systems for keeping an overview of learners with special educational needs. My guidance is to have a system where all the information exists in one place. Often, SENCos have a document in Word or something similar which lists learners and their needs. This is perfectly fine but what happens if someone leaves the school, and the admissions team don't tell the SENCo? The list is inaccurate – although in fairness as soon as you print off the list it is effectively out of date. The other issue is that these lists tend to miss out key information such as attendance, punctuality and other key data. So, the SENCo has to then get data from colleagues and try to assimilate it so that it all makes sense. Again, maybe not that hard to do but it is extra work which takes up valuable time.

It is worth exploring how you can create a list for learners with SEND where you get all the key information in one hit. The information you need already exists (apart from perhaps a description of needs) – your challenge is finding a way to capture it in one succinct format to save you time in the long run. Equally, it needs to be somewhere that colleagues can access the information so that they don't always have to come to you. This is about creating systems to raise awareness of SEND to empower others with key information and data. It is another opportunity to make sure you are not alone holding the megaphone shouting about SEND and inclusion.

There are plenty of Management Information Systems out there, but you need to consider whether they can provide all the information you need in one succinct report or format. They should be saving you time rather than creating additional administrative challenges. If you can't access the information you need it would be helpful to create your wish list and then ask someone to design a report for you which you can run periodically.

Things you may want to include in your overall report:

- Name
- Date of birth / Age
- Registration group
- Year group
- Gender
- Attendance
- Punctuality
- Ethnicity
- Pupil Premium
- SEND need type
- SEND status (K or E)
- Rewards
- Behaviour points
- Suspensions

You can add in as many categories as you want to, but the important part is analysing it all to get a whole picture and make sense of what the data is actually telling you. It might be helpful to explain the rationale behind the groups selected above.

Name

Hopefully self-explanatory, to help you identify individual learners. It may also reveal trends in families, helping you understand particular needs for children but also perhaps in the support and guidance their parents might benefit from receiving.

Date of birth / Age

Are there any particular trends emerging with learners born at particular times of the year? Equally, for some learners, is it possible that issues are developmental and a result of their age rather than them having a special educational need?

Registration/class group

Is there an imbalance between different classes in your setting? What does this mean in terms of support and guidance colleagues may need, or in terms of provision learners would benefit from? Could there be an issue in that some teachers are suggesting learners have SEND before they try different approaches in their classroom?

Year group

What support might specific year groups benefit from, given their profile? Take into account that provision needs to be dynamic: what worked for previous year groups may not be appropriate for current or future cohorts. In terms of financing, knowing that there may be a high number of learners with EHCPs joining or leaving in the future may mean budgets need to be adjusted. It may also mean that some staff whose employment is linked to specific learners may have to leave unless other roles are created.

Gender

Nationally boys make up the biggest proportion of learners with SEND. Do we notice difficulties in different ways depending on gender? Or could it be we perhaps do not notice difficulties because genders don't present in the same way?

Attendance

Are there gaps in learning because of low attendance or does an individual have a special educational need? What are you doing to support an improvement in attendance so individuals have a better chance of accessing the curriculum?

Punctuality

If learners are persistently late, what lessons are they missing and how is this impacting on their progress? For example, quite often primary schools run phonics sessions first thing. If learners are missing phonics lessons, then how might this impact on them accessing the rest of the curriculum?

Ethnicity

How does the overall ethic make-up of the SEN list compare with the school's profile? Is it that certain ethnic groups are either being over- or under–identified as having SEND?

Pupil Premium

How many of your learners with special educational needs are also in receipt of pupil premium? As a sub-group are there any particular characteristics you should be aware of so that you can better support and engage learners and their families? Equally, you may need to be mindful of the additional support learners receive through pupil premium and ensure any additional SEND provision complements what is already in place.

SEND need type

This helps us understand the profile of needs across our setting. You can compare the needs with the provision you have on offer as well as identifying professional training and support your staff may require in order to better meet needs. The other reflection for you as a SENCo is whether certain types of special educational need are more likely to be identified. This could be down to systems, staff training or specialisms the school has, so it is worth looking into the prevalence of need types compared to national, regional and local data. Are you able to clearly explain why there might be differences; for example, if you have a language unit attached to your school this might attract parents whose children have language difficulties to apply to your school. Your profile might then show a higher level of language needs compared to neighbouring schools and those regionally and nationally.

SEND status (K or E)

How many learners do you have at SEN Support and those with an Education, Health and Care Plan? You can compare this with local, regional and national data to see if your data differs (although we will explore this more later in this chapter).

Rewards

How well are your learners doing in lessons and are they more or less likely to receive rewards compared to peers? I would also reflect on high expectations and ambition for all your learners. What is the level of authenticity with which rewards are given to your learners?

Behaviour points

Similar to the above, this data might give you an indication of trends in behaviour. You can identify subjects, teachers or times of the day when issues seem to be arising. This can then be explored to better understand why behaviour deteriorates and what can be done to support learners and school staff.

Suspensions

Are suspensions disproportionately used with learners who have SEND? Re-integration meetings may also need to focus on the wider support an individual may need rather than solely reflecting on the incident that resulted in the suspension.

Explore and contrast

We know that nationally the number of learners identified as having special educational needs has been rising for quite a few years. At the time of writing the percentage of learners with an EHCP stands at 4.8% and those at SEN support is 13.6%. However, there are regional differences: the percentage of pupils with EHCPs ranges from around 5% to 4% and SEN support varies from 14.6% to 12.7%. There are even greater differences when comparing local authorities. Data also shows the difference in identification between primary and secondary settings.

Whilst comparing your SEND profile against national data may be helpful in reflecting on how your figures compare, your analysis needs to be more nuanced. It would be helpful to look at schools in the same phase as your setting and also look at data for your region and local authority. This is about being curious and posing questions rather than making judgements.

- How does our curriculum design and delivery impact on individuals accessing learning and making contributions in lessons?
- What do we do before identifying a learner has having a special educational need?
- Do we over-identify certain types of need across the school?
- Are there any types of need which we are not identifying or picking up through our assessments and observations?
- Does the perceived specialism of our setting influence parental choice when selecting schools? How does this impact on our SEND profile?

These are several questions to pose and reflect upon so that you have more of a clear and holistic understanding of how your overall context may be impacting on learners accessing the curriculum and wider learning environment. Once you feel you have a better and more secure understanding of your context then you can start thinking about more strategic leadership decisions. If these strategic leadership decisions take into account your actual context, then you can build improvements and further developments from a more secure foundation.

Reflection time

What is unique about your setting? What sets it apart from other schools in your area?

_____

_____

_____

_____

_____

_____

_____

How do your SEND figures compare with national, regional and local data? Are there any aspects that you need to look into more deeply?

_____
_____
_____
_____
_____
_____
_____

Are all staff aware of what ordinarily available / universal provision looks like and involves in your setting? Are there any training implications for you and the school?

_____
_____
_____
_____
_____
_____
_____

What does additional to and different from provision look like in your setting? How well do staff and parents understand this provision?

_____
_____
_____
_____
_____
_____
_____

What is the difference between catch-up, booster and SEND provision in your setting?

_____
_____
_____
_____
_____
_____
_____

How do you ensure that SEND provision and Pupil Premium provision complement one another and don't overwhelm individuals?

_____

_____

_____

_____

_____

_____

_____

How confident are you that there is a clear understanding of how special educational needs are identified across your setting?

_____

_____

_____

_____

_____

_____

_____

How do you feel that the profile of need across your setting impacts on individuals accessing the curriculum and wider learning environment?

_____

_____

_____

_____

_____

_____

_____

3 SEND expression of concern

SEND expressions of concern and the graduated approach

The more I visit and work with SENCos and leaders in schools, the more I am mindful of the language we use not only in our interactions but also on the documentation we have in place. Whilst some might consider this a case of semantics, I think using the phrase 'expression of concern' in SEND is more helpful than the phrase 'referral'. I have seen both terms used in schools but I do firmly believe expression of concern is the way to go.

This discussion builds on from the previous chapters and provide an opportunity for us to gain more insight and information from colleagues and other stakeholders. Systems can help us better understand the nature of the needs across our setting, as well as the endeavours our staff take in order to support learners. What we are looking at is the approach we take when concerns arise around an individual and in them accessing the curriculum and/ or the wider learning environment.

From various studies we know that SENCos are busy and time is an extremely scarce resource. We therefore need to consider the systems we develop and put in place that will help ensure our time is used effectively. One of them has to be around how we respond to staff concerns about learners accessing the curriculum or wider learning environment. What do we need to put in place to ensure that all staff take responsibility for identifying, supporting and then communicating concerns? The identifying and supporting before sharing concerns is essential before SENCos get involved. If staff aren't actively applying the graduated approach to their own practice, then it is likely that as a SENCo you are going to be doing a lot of reactive firefighting.

The other reason for developing a formalised expression of concern is that we can have a consistent response to corridor conversations or staffroom chats. In a busy world, individuals sometimes want to share information and seize any opportunity to pass it on. Quite often this results in corridor conversations where staff share concerns with the SENCo and, in doing so, believe they have communicated what they need to for you to spring into action. The concern has been passed on to the SENCo for them to look into the matter and the member of staff has done their part. The outcome is that SENCos risk returning to their office with an awful lot of information which they then need to record. At its worst there may be a reluctance to venture into the staffroom for a break because you risk coming away with more work as staff share their concerns with you.

With a formalised expression of concern, if staff come to you with a concern then your stock response can be 'Thank you for sharing your concerns, please put that down on our SEND expression of concern and we can go from there'. This then creates a clear expectation that any concern needs to be shared using the system that you have developed. It is not a personal response even though some might take it that way. It is a consistent response that starts a process of enquiry and curiosity to look into an individual's needs based on a teacher's observations. You are probably still going to get colleagues cornering you in the staffroom but at least you have a way of responding that doesn't mean you leave the staffroom with an inordinate amount of information to remember and then record back in your office.

Systems for highlighting concerns

Language matters when it comes to any system you develop in order for staff to share concerns about learners. Through supporting schools, it is something that has dawned on me more and more that any expression of concern needs to be worded carefully. Let's look at some titles (from actual schools) that seem similar but may result in totally different expectations and responses from staff.

- **Request for SENCo involvement** – this has a clear title. Staff complete the form and in doing so the form suggests that the SENCo will then become involved. This doesn't take into account what staff have done up to this point – in some cases it may be very little – but they've completed the form so the SENCo is obliged to get involved.

- **SEND Referral Form** – another clear title. If staff have a concern, then they compete a SEND referral form and the SENCo gets involved. Or does it mean the SENCo takes responsibility because the matter has been referred on to the SEND team? This all depends on the format and how you interact with staff once a referral has been made.

- **Expression of Concern** – again, pretty clear title. If staff have a concern, then they express it via the form. This may be semantics, but they are expressing a concern not referring the matter on to the SENCo. It is flagging up and sharing a concern, not just passing it fully onto the SENCo.

Whether you feel this is all down to semantics, the point is any paperwork shared is the starting point for discussing and exploring concerns. Regardless of what has been put on the form, teachers remain responsible for supporting the individual and helping them access the curriculum whether they have special educational needs or not. It is then whether you take responsibility or partner with staff to further explore and better understand what the needs of the learner might be. The subsequent conversations and reflections that take place are likely to discuss what is most helpful in knowing what the difficulties look like in the classroom, what seems to help and what doesn't.

Quality of information

There are plenty of examples of referral forms for SEND on the internet; some have a simple format over one page whilst others require several pages to be completed. My main reflection is the format you adopt needs to give you qualitative information and a clear insight into the difficulties a learner is experiencing. What I think is less helpful is when there are rows and rows of boxes to tick where staff indicate the difficulties they notice that a learner is displaying. In this instance you are getting quantity without any clear description or idea of how they impact on the learner. In many respects you are limiting what staff share with you by adopting a tick box format. Yes, it may be saving time and therefore seem appealing on that front, but consider whether it poses more questions than it answers. Ticking a box around language doesn't give you a really clear understanding of how that manifests in the classroom.

The other issue with tick boxes is where they ask staff to label / indicate what they feel the primary or main need is, staff have to tick one of the four main areas of need. What training have staff had in order to discern between, for example, a communication and interaction need and a cognition and learning need? Equally, is their assessment of need based on what is presented by the individual and seen by staff rather than what the underlying issue may actually be?

Essentially, I think it is best to keep the format really simple and stripped back. The simpler and more straightforward the form, the less likely it is that staff will complete it incorrectly or worse still, not at all. Rather than ticking boxes, we want some prose which gives us an idea of how the learner is experiencing difficulties in the learning environment. The format can also support you, the SENCo, in understanding how staff are applying the graduated approach.

If we adopt a simple and straightforward approach to our form, it might look something like this.

Space for the name of the learner and the member of staff making the expression of concern, followed by four simple boxes with space for writing.

Concern (Assess)

What are the difficulties experienced by the individual?
When do they occur or manifest in lessons or the wider learning environment?
How do they impact on the learner (and peers)?
How does the learner describe their needs / difficulties? Where and when do they feel they experience difficulties in lessons?

Support (Plan and Do)

What different teaching strategies have you adopted with the learner?
What additional resources have you shared to support the learner?
How has the learner been directly supported to help them access the curriculum?

Review

What did we notice about the impact different strategies had on the learner?
What has worked and what hasn't?
Are there any times across the week when particular strategies worked best?
How does the learner feel about the difference that the strategies and support have had on them? What did they feel worked and what was less effective?
What difficulties are still experienced by the learner?

Next steps (Assess and Plan)

Based on our learning so far, what additional teaching strategies would be most helpful to use with the learner?

What additional provision or structured intervention might the learner benefit from?

When will we revisit and review the impact of the additional strategies and support?

Do and Review

The reverse of the form could contain further boxes so you can record the impact of the next steps. This can then act as a history of need and will help if you then decide you need to seek the support of external agencies. The information recorded gives you a clear overview of need and the adjustments to practice made by the teacher, along with a review of impact and continuing difficulties.

So, on one sheet of paper you should have a clear overview of the actual difficulties experienced by the learner. You can see what the teacher has done to support and engage the learner along with the impact these strategies have had.

Adopting this format gives you the SENCo more information to go on and discuss concerns with the teacher completing the form. Instead of the issue becoming the responsibility of the SENCo, the dialogue helps ensure there is an element of partnering, with the teacher(s) remaining responsible for helping the learner access the curriculum.

It might also be helpful to indicate on the form that further high-quality teaching strategies might be suggested as part of the graduated approach. Having this explicitly on the form will help all staff understand that comleting the form is not the end of their involvement. You may need to try out different strategies to help gain a clearer understanding of underlying difficulties. So, in reality, it is not the graduated approach as a one-off cycle, but the start of several cycles and we gradually learn and understand more about individuals over time.

Include the voice of the learner

We have mentioned it earlier, but it is worth re-emphasising the importance of including the learner in this process. If we are to develop learners into confident, more independent individuals then we need to give them opportunities to contribute to their own learning and how they are supported. This also helps avoid this being a 'done unto' process where staff link strategies to what they perceive the problem to be rather than consulting the learner. Any opportunities to develop self-advocacy can only help in the long term, with individuals becoming more aware and cognisant of what will help them engage and access learning.

Reinforcing great classroom practice

The first line of intervention is in the classroom. The best type of provision to support learners is for them to have great teachers. In this respect any form or expression of concern you develop can help you reinforce and highlight the importance of high-quality teaching. It also gives you a platform to highlight what ordinarily available provision or high-quality universal provision involves in your setting.

Many local authorities now have some version of an ordinarily available provision document which outlines what they expect all schools to have in place for learners. This is yet another document for SENCos and school staff to be aware of, but it is likely to contain some really useful information. Part of the challenge is trying to highlight to staff the importance of such a document without overwhelming them. It might be worth chunking it down so that cognitive load for staff is reduced, making key information accessible and (hopefully) more likely to be read. It may well be that you just focus in on classroom practice so that you can support colleagues in being able to adapt their approaches using a variety of teaching strategies.

Model and explain rationale

Even if you keep a form simple, staff are still likely to need guidance on how to complete it so that it provides information that will be helpful to you. It is definitely worth creating a model example of what a good expression of concern would contain. You can then talk through each of the sections and explain what you might see from staff. It could be that when you introduce the form you use it as a surgery, so that each member of staff completes it for a learner for whom they might have some concerns. You can then circulate and share good practice across the staff group to reinforce their understanding of what you are looking for.

Make the rationale clear to staff. If the learner does require further support and the involvement of external agencies then you need something to share with other professionals. I liken this to going to the doctors: you can't just turn up and say 'I'm not well', as naturally the doctor would want to know more details to help them work out what might be the nature of the issue. The same is true for SENCos seeking support from external agencies; the more insightful your information and observations, then the more focused their involvement and support can be.

Remember to reinforce that when it comes to strategies we are looking for consistency over intensity. What have staff consistently used over time, rather than intensively over a week? This is important because some strategies might take a while to have an impact; equally staff may have to refine how they adopt them in their practice. Whilst we talk about being evidence-informed, we also need to be mindful that some strategies will be practice-refined and they only become effective over time as the teacher becomes more skilful in adopting and implementing them.

Describe, don't label

In the previous chapter we talked about labelling and diagnosing individuals and how this might not always be most helpful. We have already highlighted that we are looking for quality not quantity when completing this form. Equally we need to highlight the difference between a barrier or a difficulty in accessing the curriculum and a label.

The label does not inhibit or impact the learner from accessing the curriculum: it is the difficulties they experience that impact on them accessing the curriculum. When you are introducing the form, you will need to make it clear that you are looking for a clear description of the issues and difficulties experienced by the learner; you are not looking for a diagnosis from someone who is unlikely to be qualified to make that call. In your model example you can outline the type of language that is going to be helpful in further exploring what some of the underlying issues might be. For example, if the learner makes positive contributions to class discussions but then is unable to communicate the same knowledge or understanding to the page then we can explore to see whether this is due to planning, starting their work or actually writing (there are plenty more things we could explore but this is a starting point). However, if a member of staff just puts 'dyslexia' or 'dyslexic tendencies' as the issue that really doesn't tell us much at all.

Describing the difficulties that learners experience then helps us to explore what some of the barriers might be. If we know what a particular barrier is then we can take steps to address and remove it or help the learner to overcome it. If it is auditory memory, we can supply notes or a tick list. If they use limited vocabulary, then we can pre-teach and share additional vocabulary that they can use in their work, and we can reinforce this during the lesson. All of this helps us reinforce the social model of disability rather than the medical model. What are the barriers and what can we do as professionals to remove them or minimise the negative impact they are having?

The role of other leaders

Another consideration here relates to the work and practices of other leaders in your setting. It is worth considering the role middle leaders play in discussing concerns around individual learners. This may be down to the culture of your setting, but consider how they are involved in discussions before any concerns reach you. In an ideal world, departmental or phase meetings will have an element of discussion around learners who may be causing concern and then exploring what might work for them.

Essentially, how many conversations have taken place before the issue has been passed on to you? What we want is for our middle leaders to discuss pedagogy and practice with their teams. Any issues can be discussed with additional strategies being shared so that staff can try out different approaches which will hopefully address the issue. If this is happening, then we should have some degree of confidence that staff are taking responsibility for learners before they involve you. After all, in the classroom staff often have a list of things learners can do before they call on support from the teacher, e.g. brain, book, board, buddy. The same is true for your colleagues. How are they helping themselves before seeking your help and support?

As this is around culture, it may be that you have some work to undertake with middle leaders so that they are fully aware of your expectations. This may take some time because the culture and working patterns weren't established overnight, and nor will they change overnight, so there will be a need for continuous reinforcement of expectations on your part. You have the Teachers' Standards to also support your request for staff to consider possible difficulties and adapt their teaching accordingly. You are not asking them to do anything over and above that which is outlined in the Teachers' Standards.

Balancing support and challenge

You are a SENCo: you want to help other people but you only have so many hours in the day along with finite levels of energy and resources. There is a risk that you provide so much support that you end up doing the work for colleagues. In your efforts to help and support you end up doing the work *for* rather than *with* colleagues. What are they learning from this process if you are always solving the issues or dealing with the problems they are experiencing?

The flipside to this is that you challenge staff to meet the needs of learners without giving them adequate support or guidance. This then creates a situation where you are doing 'to' staff. It might create heightened anxiety amongst colleagues because you are asking them to do something which they might feel ill-equipped or not sufficiently skilled to do. One of the possible outcomes is that staff then simply don't complete any expressions of concern because they just don't know how or what language to use or they don't want to get it wrong. The problem for you as a SENCo would then be that you think 'everything is fine, no concerns, so all is good' when the reality is learners aren't accessing the curriculum as well as they might and things aren't getting any better.

It is perfectly fine to make your expectations clear but the challenge for you as a leader is to find the right equilibrium between support and challenge. This is about working with colleagues. Yes, you have introduced the challenge of asking for concerns to be shared and completed in a particular format. You have however provided guidance, examples of what good concerns look like and shared great teaching strategies. You can also talk through concerns when you receive them so you create dialogue and shared responsibility rather than it being more transactional with everything then being for you to do.

Parental input to the graduated approach

If concerns persist despite a cycle or cycles of assess, plan, do and review then it would be helpful to consult with parents. (You can of course consult with parents earlier but it might be helpful to share what you have done to address concerns in the first instance.)

Concerns at school along with strategies used can be shared with parents. What do they see at home? Do they have any strategies that they use which are effective? These can then be collated to have a clearer understanding of the difficulties experienced by the individual along with useful strategies.

These conversations with parents can also reveal more about an individual's stages of development as well as family history. It could be that significant events have had an impact on an individual which might explain why they are now experiencing difficulties. This is another opportunity to find out more about the holistic individual so that any subsequent strategies or support can focus more on underlying needs. It is also an opportunity to ensure consistency between home and school.

Developing a picture of need over time

The other benefit of having a structured and purposeful expression of concern is that you can develop an understanding of needs over time. If several staff have completed expressions of concern, then you can see how needs are evolving and you are then able to develop a clearer understanding of possible underlying issues. This information is then extremely helpful in understanding needs and wondering what might be the most appropriate way to support the learner.

Signposting support for professional learning

Over time you are likely to receive several expressions of concern that have been completed by staff. Themes may well start to appear which may indicate issues with staff confidence or practice when it comes to particular types of need. These themes can be collated, shared and discussed with senior colleagues to highlight potential focus areas for professional development and learning. It may also be that the absence of specific strategies might indicate that staff would benefit from training linked to this area of need.

Avoid becoming a rescuer

This is directly linked to the above and explores support and challenge in more depth and in a working social context. Stephen Karpman proposed a model for social interaction in 1968 calling it the 'drama triangle'. It looks at three different roles that can be played out during interactions. These being the persecutor, rescuer and victim.

Some things to consider before we go any further. We know that SENCos are often nurturing individuals who want to help, want to support colleagues and want to do their utmost so that learners with SEND get the best possible educational experience. We also know that SENCos are often time poor with competing priorities and often feel rushed or pressured to complete key tasks across their working week.

With the above points in mind, we need to be mindful of the actual reason why an expression of concern form was introduced in the first place. The expression of concern was introduced because we need to know how and where a learner experiences difficulties accessing the curriculum and wider learning environment. This will help us better understand an individual but also give external agencies useful information so that they can focus on specific issues rather than general concerns.

We therefore need to be resolute when it comes to maintaining expectations and standards when expressions of concern are given to us. If a concern doesn't meet the clear standards we set out, then we need to give it back. We may talk it through in the first instance and do some modelling, but we need to ensure the member of staff retains responsibility for completing the form. This is after all a concern they have so they have a responsibility to clearly and coherently articulate what the issues are and what they have done to address them in the first instance. The teacher is the first line of intervention in the classroom, so we need to gain their insight.

If we fall into the rescuer mode and accept concerns that aren't up to expectations then we risk the following:

- **More work:** we create more work for ourselves because instead of challenging colleagues, we are doing what they should have done.

- **Bottlenecks** are created because everything then has to go through the SENCo because staff are not confident or inclined to complete concerns with the necessary information. You have then created more work for yourself because in helping you have actually created a dependency culture.

- **Disempowering** and possibly de-skilling colleagues because you are doing work that might have supported self-reflection and professional learning, had they done it themselves. You might also create 'victims' who complain about learners not engaging but do nothing about it because you are going to 'rescue' them.

- **Limiting what others could do** because the solutions or ways forward are based on your knowledge and experience rather than potentially more creative ways forward which colleagues might come up with. It is therefore important to be clear that what you suggest are just some examples and that others might be equally effective. For this point, ask for staff to share their ideas before you share yours. If you go first then others might be reluctant to share their own ideas because you have already said what is likely to work.

- **Create 'persecutors'**: colleagues criticise your suggested strategies because they simply don't work. Your 'help' is not what they want; they are competent practitioners with a variety of strategies they can use. They want guidance and discussion not 'rescuing'.

Reflection time

How do staff share any concerns about learners with you? How does this impact on your workload?

_____
_____
_____
_____
_____
_____
_____

What will a good expression of concern look like and what key information would you want it to contain?

_____
_____
_____
_____
_____
_____
_____

How does your expression of concern link to the language your school uses around effective teaching and learning? Are any changes needed so your form aligns with this pedagogy?

_____
_____
_____
_____
_____
_____
_____

What work do I need to undertake with middle leaders so they can support staff before a concern is completed?

_____
_____
_____
_____
_____
_____
_____

When you receive a concern, what is your initial response to the member of staff? Does the member of staff retain responsibility or is this something you tend to assume?

_____
_____
_____
_____
_____
_____
_____

What will professional challenge look and sound like when staff share concerns without adding helpful, qualitative information and observations?

_____
_____
_____
_____
_____
_____
_____

What steps do you need to take in order to facilitate parental input into the graduated approach?

_____
_____
_____
_____
_____
_____
_____

What leadership actions do I need to undertake in order to establish and embed an expression of concern system?

_____
_____
_____
_____
_____
_____

Who else can review expressions of concern and talk through what they feel could be added by teachers? How might you give guidance and feedback to staff?

_____
_____
_____
_____
_____
_____
_____

4 Fresh eyes on provision

This links us back to the first chapter on vision when you might hear statements like 'But we've always done it like this!' or worse '[name of the previous person in your role] found that this system worked best for the school'. So, if you're new to the role or new to the school you may encounter some resistance to change or worse still, some passive aggressive comments, possibly because for some, change means uncertainty. You also need to bear in mind that some people have a reputation at stake, so their involvement is making you question the need for change. If things change, how will it impact on their standing in the team and across the school? This is not just about changes to what happens at school – this is changing the status quo for some individuals, which means you are likely to get emotional or political responses as opposed to rational ones. That shouldn't deter you from changing things; it is just a factor to be aware of as any future plans might be impacted on by individual responses and how an individual might then influence the responses of the rest of the team or other staff around the school.

Remember, any changes need to link back to your vision: the greater clarity around your vision, the easier it will be to link developments back to why they are necessary. Our vision is what we can anchor our changes around to give them greater purpose and meaning. Your challenge as a leader is in articulating the ongoing link between new ways of working and how they support progress to the vision. This will give staff more confidence in it.

What we as SENCos need to grasp and then communicate is that contexts have changed, as have the needs of learners we are dealing with. This is something that is coming across loud and clear in all the schools I visit. So, if things are different, needs are more complex, support from frontline agencies possibly less available than it was, then we need to do something differently. What got the school to where it is now will not be adequate for helping it progress in the future. If we refer back to Chapter 1, outcomes for SEND learners are not good nor have they shown any meaningful improvement, so we need new habits, new behaviours, new ways of thinking and new/different approaches in the classroom.

SEND Code of Practice legacy issue

Part of our challenge is what I would best describe as a legacy issue when the SEND Code of Practice was changed back in 2014. Some areas took the steps to encourage schools to develop whole school provision maps to outline waves or tiers of provision across their school. There's absolutely nothing wrong with this; I think it is useful to have a clear understanding of the provision available across your school. The problem is that very few got updated. What you see are some provisions listed that haven't run for years. The result is nobody really has a clear understanding of the overall additional support and provision available across the school. The other problem is you have a provision that might help learners, but you no longer have members of staff who can deliver the provision.

If you do have this whole school provision map in place, then you have two choices. You can either ignore it and confine it to the bin or you can review and update it. If you choose to renew it, then it would be helpful to do this with colleagues in different roles across the school, so you get a holistic overview of 'different from and additional to' provision. The colleagues in question might be the Pupil Premium lead, pastoral leads or heads of phase or subjects. Basically, you are liaising with anyone who offers additional support across the school. Once you have your updated whole school provision map then you have a starting point. A starting point is to be curious about why certain activities are taking place across the school as well as gaining an understanding as to who oversees and quality assures them.

Take a graduated approach

When you are developing your list of provision it might be helpful to take a graduated approach. The provision can be ordered so staff can understand what order they might follow in. For instance, what follows on from great classroom practice might be a small group intervention. If the small group intervention is not working, then using the assess, plan, do and review approach we can identify a more intensive provision that is appropriate for the individual. Having the list ordered can also help avoid situations where a learner goes from whole class support to one-to-one provision. This might be appropriate in some situations, but it's worth considering if another intervention could come before that intensive (and generally more expensive) provision.

Lead time for external support

Another consideration you might take into account when developing your list of additional provision relates to the lead time for specific types of external support. If we know that occupational therapy visits are infrequent then we may need to consider what in-house provision we need to develop in order to support learners whilst we wait for external agencies to get engaged.

This links in with a graduated approach again, in that we are looking to support learners before any issues escalate but we are also gathering evidence at the same time. This evidence then helps support any referral we do make to external agencies. We can also ensure that when engaged, these external agencies come up with guidance, advice and strategies over and above that which you have already tried. If these agencies are deemed to be specialists, then we need to challenge them by putting in place robust support before engaging them. This then removes the likelihood that they will make recommendations which are basic because the school has already put them in place. The attitude to take is that if these are specialists, they need to be giving you advice you don't already know or haven't thought of. If they can't do that then you may need to look elsewhere for better support and guidance.

Make it accessible and understood by all

One of the drawbacks of just having a list of additional provision is some staff still don't really know what is involved and which learners might benefit from accessing the provision. What you can do is turn your list into a catalogue of provision, with clear expected outcomes and the types of learners that would most benefit from the provision.

The other reason for developing this catalogue with the extra detail is that it can support more informed decision-making. You are removing some of the 'it's an additional provision, the learner is not making progress so let's try it'. Instead, what you have is a clear overview of provision that staff can consider when discussing the needs of individuals or groups of learners. If we know that some learners are having difficulties understanding instructions, for example, then we can go to the communication and interaction sections and look at any provision we offer for receptive language (it could also be a comprehension issue which might then need cognition and learning provision). Again, consider what the needs of the cohort are and what specifically your school can offer in order to support them in accessing the curriculum and functioning in the wider learning environment.

Finally, the other reason for having a catalogue of additional provision which is clearly understood is that it can support informed decision-making in the absence of the SENCo. It is great for the SENCo to be involved in discussions around appropriate support for individuals but there will be occasions when you just don't have the time to attend meetings. Your colleagues can then use the catalogue to inform the most appropriate next steps when it comes to supporting an individual. It also helps ensure that staff don't just focus on the provisions they oversee. For instance, in a secondary school you may have a pastoral meeting where behaviour is being spoken about. Rather than go down a punitive approach, if staff consider the learner's underlying needs then a more targeted provision could be identified to best support the individual and the difficulties they are actually experiencing.

Tracking and monitoring

The next action to take is to look into each provision you have on your list and carry out some basic checks. Some simple actions would be:

- Is the intervention evidence informed or designed in-house?

- Are expected outcomes clear? Do you know what improvements you will see if learners access the intervention? (If these aren't tight then success can be subjective.)

- Do you have a baseline from which you can objectively measure progress? How do you capture entry and exit data?

- Is the learning from these interventions being used back in classrooms?

- Are staff aware of how they can reinforce the learning from interventions through their classroom practices?

- How do intervention leaders record session by session progress, including qualitative observations?

- Are intervention leaders qualified to deliver the intervention? When did they last have update training?

- Are interventions being delivered with fidelity to the programme? You will need to undertake drop-ins to see if content is being delivered as per the programme guidance.

Really, what we are doing here is understanding the additional provisions on offer, whether they are fit for purpose and then stripping back any provision that can't be measured or does not lead to positive outcomes for the majority of learners accessing them. The mantra we need to adopt when we are undertaking reviews like this is 'fact not anecdote'. What are the facts and data telling us about the additional provision we are currently running? This might also include exploring the voice of the learner to see what their experience has been having accessed an intervention. What we can't go on are statements like 'They seem happier' or 'They look more confident'. We have to go on objective facts, not subjective views which might be influenced by the staff delivering the intervention itself.

Review and quality assure

Just as you undertake learning walks and lesson drop-ins to get an insight into the experience of the learners in the classroom, you also need to do the same for interventions. Doing this is an opportunity to mentor and coach your team so that delivery improves over time, but equally an opportunity to help ensure that programmes are delivered as they are intended to be. This focuses on fidelity to the programme and helping avoid staff compromising the impact because they feel something should be delivered differently to what the programme says. That is not to say we don't adapt and alter provision over time, but it is done as a collective reflection and review activity rather than down to the whim of an individual.

Are we sticking to time?

Another key area to monitor is the length of time an intervention is meant to be delivered for. If a session is designed for 30 minutes, then how confident are you that the full 30 minutes are being used effectively to deliver the intervention? Through your learning walks you can gain an understanding of whether the full time is used or whether learners are given 'golden time' because they have been good and focused for 20 minutes. You can imagine reviewing some interventions and wondering why they aren't having the impact you thought but then realising they have only been delivered for two-thirds of the intended time!

Demand-led not supply-led

Before I became a SENCo, I was a business studies teacher – which I know happens to be the best subject ever! One of the things my subject teaching taught me was if we have a demand-led approach, we can better meet the needs of our customers, who in this case our learners. If we have a supply-led approach, then we risk selling or providing something that our learners don't want or need. This then puts us in a situation where we are trying to support with the wrong tools and wrong provision.

Potentially this could put some of our learners off because we simply aren't supporting them in the way they actually need to be supported. We are not utilising the lived experience and voice of the learner to give us feedback on what they feel works. At its worst we may see a deterioration in behaviour because learners really do not want to attend the additional provision, as in their eyes it is just not right for them. This may include some reflection as to whether your provision is age-appropriate for your learners.

Your provision therefore needs to be based around the actual needs of your current (and future) cohort. In a simple compare and contrast activity, look at your biggest areas of need and then look at the provision you have in place. Does your setting have provision in place to meet current needs? If the answer is no, then you have gaps that need your leadership attention and focus. Before you do this undertaking, there are some other considerations you need to take into account.

Curriculum design

A key consideration is whether you need to communicate with other leaders in your setting to consider the appropriateness of the school's curriculum. This can include reviewing opportunities across the curriculum to develop skills as well as knowledge. It may also include reflections on pacing and whether there are opportunities for over-learning and consolidation so that learning becomes more secure.

Part of the analysis needs to focus in on what you want your learners to acquire in terms of knowledge and skills. You then need to track back and consider what the potential barriers are going to be for cohorts. Adaptations can then be made to the curriculum content so that learners are not disadvantaged by any assumptions made when it comes to content and sequencing.

Could or should this be done in the classroom?

Could or should certain types of provision be delivered in the classroom? It is really important at this stage for you to have confidence in the message you have communicated and have continued to reinforce about what high-quality teaching looks like and involves in the classroom. If you have made it really clear, if you have shared and celebrated good practice, then all your staff will have a clear understanding of the overall expectations you and the school has for them in terms of how they support and engage learners in the classroom.

If there is a significant need across a class or year group or even the school, then you need to consider how you are adapting your first line of intervention in order to support access and engagement to the curriculum. You need to think carefully about the presenting needs and then what pedagogy can be adopted in order to better meet the needs of these learners. For example, we know that speech, language and communication is a significant need, especially in early years and Key Stage 1. There therefore needs to be a focus on how language and communication is explicitly developed throughout the school day and in every lesson. Instead of assuming language is in place or that learners know how to speak and listen to one another we need to scaffold opportunities and constantly reinforce and then develop it when we interact with our learners. First and foremost, this needs to be done in the classroom before we start thinking about taking learners out for additional provision.

An additional consideration here is any effects resulting from learners leaving the classroom. What impact does that have on the learning they are missing? Or on their self-esteem and how they feel they are perceived by their peers. Equally, how will this impact on the teacher supporting the learners when they return to the classroom? Is there an additional challenge on the teacher to make sure missed learning is caught up without then overloading the individual?

Anticipatory

When you are considering what additional provision for your current cohort you can also consider what will be necessary in the future. The Equality Act 2010 has an anticipatory element so schools need to think about future cohorts. Essentially, the consideration is what reasonable adjustments need to be made in advance so that we do not disadvantage learners who have or may have SEND. The leadership action here is to liaise with feeder settings, analysing data and discussing the presenting needs along with strategies and approaches that have been effective in supporting learners. This can then help identify additional gaps in your existing provision and support strategic planning.

If you develop positive links with your feeder settings, then you may well seek opportunities to benefit from their expertise. The additional provision that they have developed can be shared with your own setting (possibly adapted so that it is age-appropriate). The experts from the feeder settings can upskill your staff and share effective strategies. An example of this might relate to reading. Not many secondary staff know how to teach reading nor are they necessarily aware of phonics. Some professional learning can then be undertaken to support teaching staff to focus on reading approaches so that learners have a better chance of accessing the curriculum on transition to Key Stage 3.

What do you need now? What needs to be developed over time?

You have undertaken your compare and contrast activity, looking at needs and comparing it to the provision you currently have on offer. You have also spoken with colleagues across the school to ensure that your list reflects a whole school offer. Your next step is undertaking a gap analysis to identify what you don't have in place. From this analysis, you can construct a list detailing all the provision you think will be necessary.

Your next steps will involve researching programmes and different types of support that can address your gaps in provision. The EEF is always a good starting point as the research has already been undertaken on specific programmes. The benefits, conclusions and limitations of the studies can also give you an idea of whether these programmes may be appropriate for your setting. It can also guide you as to what you need to do in order for the programme to be as effective as possible. You can also approach suppliers of interventions directly, but do so bearing in mind they are commercial organisations. If their claims of progress and impact seem astonishing, then perhaps dig a little deeper and ask for research findings or evidence from schools already using the provision (making sure they don't receive any incentive for referrals).

Once you have your list of desired additional provision, then you will need to undertake a priority exercise. What is the most pressing issue in your setting that your existing provision is not catering for? Again, through discussions with other leaders a list of interventions can be developed in a hierarchical order. You can then plan for how you are going to develop the additional provision in your setting. There is also going to be a financial cost of introducing new provision so this may well affect your decision as to what you can afford to put in place in the immediate future.

Strategic development of staff

Using the list of additional provision you identified through your compare and contrast activity, you can then add in another dimension, looking at the existing skills and qualifications of the staff you have in your team and across the school. Draw up a matrix listing the provision you need, the list of trained staff able to deliver that provision and a date when they were trained or last had refresher training for that provision.

This matrix then gives you an idea of the existing skills you can immediately draw upon and then the skills you need to develop or get people trained in. This may also trigger some debate around whether your existing staff can be trained or whether you need to recruit staff with a specific skills set. This then gives you short-term actions and then longer-term actions in that some training may take longer to put in place or it may take time to recruit the right individuals.

Ensuring there is accommodation for the interventions

This is a challenge for many schools, as there are lots of children to support and additional interventions to run but limited space in which to do so. Difficult choices need to be made, and it often feels like a challenging game of solitaire. If you don't have the right accommodation, you might be limiting the impact of the intervention or wasting time with staff hunting round for a spare room. If it is decided that the intervention needs to run, then you need to identify a suitable space for it to take place so the intervention lead can focus on delivering content to the learners. The learners can focus on what is being delivered instead of perhaps being distracted by people passing by them in the corridor or feeling claustrophobic because they are in a glorified cupboard with no windows.

The corridor often ends up being the last resort or final option that schools often arrive at. But is it the right choice? I think there is a double consideration for us here. How many distractions take place because corridors tend to have people moving about in them even during lesson time? The other consideration is the impact on the self-esteem of the individual or group of individuals. You are highly visible in the corridor and most importantly, you are not in the classroom so how might that affect them? I know it is often a last resort, but it might be worth undertaking a pupil voice activity to understand how they feel about it. It might be they are not bothered in the slightest, but it is definitely worth looking into.

Additional provision is not just for SEND

Finance has been mentioned above; it is a scarce resource and often a commodity SENCos see little of. The point here is that we have talked about additional provision, but not all learners accessing it are going to have SEND. Indeed, if we identify issues early and ensure there is prompt intervention to support the individual then they may not need to go on the SEND list. With this in mind and taking a whole school approach, not all provision should be paid for out of the SEND budget.

Part of your analysis can include producing a list of all the learners who have accessed additional provision over an academic year. How many of the learners are in receipt of pupil premium or not identified as SEND? You can build the case that provision adopts an 'inclusion for all' approach. If it is effective, then it will support learners before their needs escalate. To this end, the funding should come from across the school because it is having a wider impact beyond just those learners with SEND.

Reflection time

Take some time here to jot down a couple of sentences about the provision you have across your setting.

Do you have a clear understanding of all the 'different from and additional to' provision that is available across your setting?

_____
_____
_____
_____
_____
_____
_____

Is the current provision in place across your setting meeting the needs of all learners? What gaps are there?

_____
_____
_____
_____
_____
_____
_____

What provision should be delivered in the classroom and how will you support colleagues in delivering on this?

_____
_____
_____
_____
_____
_____
_____

Who can help you research and identify additional provision that will further develop and improve what you offer in your setting?

_____
_____
_____
_____
_____
_____
_____

What changes or adaptations to processes for learners being placed on additional provision across your setting are necessary so that they do not completely rely on the SENCo's involvement?

_____
_____
_____
_____
_____
_____
_____

What is going to be your justification for seeking funding from other budgets in order to further develop provision across your setting?

_____
_____
_____
_____
_____
_____
_____

Which agencies or professionals can you work with to help you establish clear baselines and quality assurance measures for each type of provision?

_____
_____
_____
_____
_____
_____
_____

5 School systems

Layers and layers

There is a great book called *Why do I need a teacher when I've got Google?* by Ian Gilbert. It is a really interesting read with insightful views into how schools operate. One of the areas that gets attention is the layering of support in schools. There is a tendency to add layers of support and then add even more layers of support without ever really being cognisant of the difference each layer is making. When results go well, staff congratulate themselves; when results don't go so well it is often blamed on cohort variation.

Having visited and supported multiple schools it is evident to me that extra layers and initiatives are added into school systems. Each layer added with the best intentions and a clear objective to improve rates of progress or engagement across the curriculum. What schools are often unable to understand, or measure, is the difference each layer of support is actually having on individuals and groups of learners. What is potentially happening is that some schools are overworking staff by getting them to do more and more in order to boost the performance of learners.

Cynically, if we think about school practices around examination times, we see this layering of support in its extreme. After school classes are put in place, breakfast booster clubs, Saturday sessions, Easter revision classes. All the time, more and more layers are put in place without knowing the difference each individual layer is actually making. We see that we are working hard but not necessarily effectively. If we refer back to our chapter on provision, then what is 'different from and additional to' the practices which take place every day? Are we simply doing more of the same but expecting different results?

The key question is: if we had to take away one layer of support, which one would it be? What systems do we have in place that would give us objective data and the confidence that we have made the right decision? In a time of tightening budgets, we need to have systems in place that let us know the efficacy of the support and additional provision we have in place across our setting.

Tsunami or focused support?

In a high-stakes assessment system, there is a focus on ensuring all learners reach age-related expectations or in supporting them to reach the magic number 4 or 5 in their GCSEs (or whatever is needed to gain a pass in equivalent qualifications). Anyone who is not meeting the expected standard is targeted for additional support and placed on an intervention, or in some cases, several interventions. Highlighting the intervention-/provision-led approach we see learners accessing several interventions at the same time. In extreme cases, some learners are spending a significant percentage of time outside of the classroom in order to try and help them catch up whilst all the time they are missing out on what their peers are learning. You have to wonder whether the gaps in learning are being exacerbated by spending such a significant amount of time outside of lessons with their peers.

Impact of support on the learner

Part of the reflection here needs to consider the impact on the learner and how they feel about accessing so many different interventions. There may well be some impact on their self-esteem as they leave the classroom again for more 'help'.

The other consideration is how the learner is making sense of all the additional support so they are cognisant of how they are going to use their new learning back in the classroom and in any examination. There is a real risk that unless intervention leads are explicitly linking content to classroom learning, then what happens in an intervention will be compartmentalised.

You can imagine a GCSE student who is borderline and may have had little support over the years because they were doing OK. All of a sudden, discussions in senior meetings identify them as someone who needs support or, more cynically, the school needs them to do better for GCSE scores. Anyway, the individual is then the target of several subject leads who want to 'help'. You can imagine that in some situations a learner has gone from very little support to a tsunami of support which may well be overwhelming. They probably need support to help them make sense of all the support they are suddenly receiving.

Clear communication systems

In order to mitigate against intervention overload there needs to be clarity around the priorities for individual learners. Key staff (such as SENCo, subject leads, pastoral leads, Pupil Premium leads) need to communicate in order to coordinate the support that needs to be put in place for an individual learner (a similar approach to that outlined in the previous chapter). There may need to be some negotiation around what support needs to happen first. Without this co-ordinated approach you risk staff working in silos and doing what they think is best for an individual without having oversight of the bigger picture.

If you take a coordinated approach then you can share knowledge of individual learners, develop a clearer understanding of where they might be experiencing difficulties and then prioritise what needs to happen first. You can also agree dates for progress updates so you can discuss how things are going, whether changes need to be made or whether a different approach is needed altogether. This co-ordinated approach might also support your setting in working with a wider group of learners, because support is not then concentrated on just a few.

Identifying keyworkers

Another consideration relates to who is actually taking responsibility to make sure the learner is OK and is accessing support as they should. You run the risk of everyone being responsible and in doing so no one is responsible because they all think their colleagues are seeing to it. The other consideration is that if you don't assign staff to work with individual learners, then you might risk anyone that has been identified with SEND being assigned to the SENCo. This might not seem an issue, but does it create an equitable split of responsibility and workload?

If you co-ordinate support across keyworkers you can be more responsive and more agile in how all staff are working. Weekly or fortnightly review meetings give an opportunity to talk through progress and any barriers to engagement, and then to explore possible adjustments to what support is actually needed.

What's our starting point?

In the 'Fresh eyes on provision' chapter we talked about the need for establishing an objective starting point. This has really got to be the case for any additional provision we put in place. We need to be clear about the gaps in learning or development so that we can objectively measure any progress made. We need to be clear that progress is based on fact and not anecdote.

We need to consider what the starting point is for the learner before they access additional provision. This might involve some baseline or undertaking an additional assessment to give us an objective, data-based baseline. Different provisions may have different assessments but might involve some of the following examples (not exhaustive, you can probably come up with lots more).

Social, Emotional and Mental Health

- Boxall profile
- Strengths and Difficulties Questionnaire (SDQ)
- Pupil Attitudes to Self and School survey (PASS)

Cognition and Learning

- New Group Reading Test (NGRT)
- Cognitive Ability Test (CAT)

Communication and Interaction

- Nuffield Early Language Intervention (NELI)
- WellCom

There are plenty of other assessments available on the market, but these are a starting point to consider and reflect about what you have in place in order to establish a baseline for learners.

Your starting point is then a reliable assessment which should provide you with robust data which you can then objectively measure progress against.

Even if you don't have access to any of the above assessments, you need to think about establishing a secure starting point. Without a clear starting point any progress is going to be subjective. The other issue is that you may overestimate or underestimate progress which is then going to influence future decision-making regarding support for an individual.

Standardise tracking for interventions

One thing that will help ensure you have a handle on the difference each of the interventions is making is by standardising your tracking systems. This might seem obvious, but I have visited so many schools where each individual intervention has its own tracking which doesn't tie in with others. In a few settings, interventions were recorded in diaries (which is probably also a GDPR issue), which then begs the question on how the information can be analysed.

What you then have is several different tracking systems which don't really give consistent information, making it extremely hard to capture on an overall database. You end up with information or if you are lucky, 'data' which is challenging to compare.

We have looked at some of the standard information we would want but it is worth looking at it again so you can develop a standard tracking document. Again, you are looking for a simple and straightforward approach so that anyone using it is less likely to make mistakes.

Broaden the baseline

One thing I think that is important is looking at the holistic development of an individual. It might be that a 6-week intervention doesn't necessarily lead to an improved reading age. However, what we might see is an improvement in punctuality as the learner gradually feels more confident about attending school because they can access and understand what is happening in lessons a little more.

You have an opportunity to look holistically at the individual once you have put additional provision in place. Your baseline can then extend to punctuality, attendance, rewards, behaviour points, suspensions and so on. What you might then see is the wider impact of additional provision. I think this is a useful lens to look through because for some learners you aren't going to have an immediate turnaround. Despite having high expectations there will be some learners who don't make the progress you might expect. What you might however see is a broader impact on their overall engagement and conduct around the school setting.

It could be that by targeting your support you are addressing some of the underlying anxieties which then makes it possible for progress to be made at a later date.

Checking back to make sure progress is secure

A while back (and recently in some settings) there was a lot of talk around learners making rapid and sustained progress. I'll lay my cards on the table at this point, I think 'rapid and sustained' is an oxymoron. I think you can have rapid progress, and you can have sustained progress, but rarely both together. Rapid to me means: intensive support, high rates of progress – and then a decline in progress because you have taken the support away. Sustained on the other hand is where you have measured and understood needs, targeted support and then gradually removed the scaffolding so that progress is more secure.

With the above in mind, it is worth considering how you check in with learners a period of time after the additional provision has ceased. You need to know the longevity of the progress and you need to know whether the new learning has stuck. It might then be worth factoring in a 3-month check-in with learners to see just how well they are doing. This might involve views from staff in the classroom, parental insights and the voice of the learner themselves. This is obviously extra work, but it will give you a clear insight into which of your provisions really make a long-term impact for your learners.

Success through other interventions

Let's briefly return to layers and the importance of rationalising support. One thing you need to think about is that you might believe learners have made progress on an intervention, but could it actually be as the result of another intervention? I'll give you an example of what I mean. You place a learner on several interventions including reading comprehension and numeracy. It could be that the reading comprehension intervention is not actually that effective, but because the numeracy intervention focuses on understanding the wording in questions, you see an improvement in comprehension.

This then makes it all the more important to really consider the diet of interventions you put in place for learners. If you (you as in you and other staff in your setting) get it wrong, then you might end up with a skewed understanding of the impact individual interventions are having on learners. Worse still, if you have to rationalise your offer you may end up ceasing to offer what are actually effective interventions.

Reflection time

How confident are you in your school systems to help you identify the difference each layer of support is making for individuals? What might you do differently?

_____
_____
_____
_____
_____
_____
_____

What communication systems are in place to help avoid school staff working in silos and avoid overloading learners with support?

_____
_____
_____
_____
_____
_____
_____

Do all interventions have a clear baseline so that progress can be objectively measured? What may need to be introduced for each intervention?

_____
_____
_____
_____
_____
_____
_____

What measures do you use to gauge whether additional support has been effective and impactful on learners?

_____

_____

_____

_____

_____

_____

_____

How confident are you that additional support has a lasting impact on learners and what systems do you have in place to evidence lasting impact?

_____

_____

_____

_____

_____

_____

_____

6 Data and information

Data-rich and information-rich?

There is no denying that schools are awash with data, whether it be teacher assessments, data from in-house screening or from formal examinations. The question is, how do we use it to inform our approaches to teaching and learning to help us understand the underlying needs of individual learners? I am going to be blunt here and say in a lot of cases data goes to waste and is not used in a judicious manner to inform approaches in the classroom and wider learning environment. What we have is data-rich settings which are information-poor. It is often assumed that staff understand what data scores mean and use them to adapt their approaches in the classroom. In a lot of cases that simply isn't true and isn't happening or isn't happening with a consistent understanding around what the data means.

If we were to undertake a cost-benefit analysis of getting data by carrying out assessments in schools, I would suspect the costs would possibly outweigh the benefits. I would argue that there are missed opportunities and benefits which might otherwise improve how staff understand and use such data. We will return to this later on in the chapter. The first thing to think about is what we hope to get from the data and how it will help us in working with our learners, especially those with SEND.

Storing assessment data

A key consideration relates to where you store data so that it is accessible for all staff. Just by placing information on the shared area or on the school's Management Information System (MIS) does not mean that staff will access it. Part of the challenge is in making sure that data is an integral part of teaching practice, so it is used to support reflection and inform lesson planning and teaching delivery. For that to happen, staff need to have access to it *and* understand what it means. In terms of accessing it, it might be interesting to see how many clicks you need to make in order to find and access the data you want. If staff have to go through several folders, then at what point will they give up? I liken this process to online shopping, any more than two clicks and you are less likely to make a purchase. So, how many clicks do your staff have to make?

Analysis and interpretation

Let's focus on literacy and cognitive assessments (but the same will be true for other types of assessment). Schools receive a wealth of data – lots of spreadsheets or tables detailing scores achieved by individuals. The question is what then happens with this data? Is it placed on the shared area or MIS or linked to a class marksheet for staff to refer to? If that is all that is done and staff don't actually refer back to it, then my cost benefit point stands true.

We need to take the data and really analyse and interpret it, so we understand what it means for learners accessing the curriculum. This action then needs to be followed up by working with all staff, so they understand what the data actually means. We need to interpret the data and apply it to learners and how it will impact on them in the classroom. There is an opportunity to really utilise data and make better use of it but there is going to be some work involved in that. This work is not solely down to the SENCo but will rely on your leadership to get other leaders onboard to plan and undertake action.

Some of your actions may involve working with the data lead so there is consistency in how data is presented and shared with staff. There also needs to be clarity over what actions you expect staff to take once they have key data.

You might also liaise with the CPD lead in order to arrange for staff training around a particular issue raised by an analysis of data. For instance, if your reading assessment data reveals there is an issue with comprehension, then you need to communicate this and staff need to learn about different strategies they can use to support reading comprehension. In the first instance, before you leap to putting in place a suite of interventions, you need to think about the high-quality teaching approaches you can use to support access and engagement. In short, what are you and all of your staff doing consistently at a whole school level?

Another approach you could take is by attending departmental or phase meetings to discuss assessment scores and link it back to high-quality teaching and access to the curriculum. If you adopt this approach, you might then get middle leaders to use that as a line of inquiry when progress or behaviour concerns arise. What is the data telling you? How are staff in your team using it to inform and adapt their teaching?

So what?

This is not intended to be belligerent in any way but where schools put assessment scores on their MIS for staff to access, my question is 'So what?'. Who actually understands the data? Who knows what it means for learners accessing the curriculum? We can draw on a couple of examples to help reinforce the point.

Reading ages by themselves can mean very little. Yes, they tell you that an individual might have a reading age of 7 years and 5 months, but what does that actually mean? You might have several learners with the same reading age in your class but that doesn't mean they read and understand text in the same way. The reading age alone doesn't tell you about the strength of decoding or the degree of comprehension. The data that is shared therefore needs to be more specific or detailed in order to give an understanding about possible difficulties with reading so that you support and guide staff with their classroom practices. In many cases this will be sharing decoding and comprehension scores instead of reading ages. Two pieces of useful data which can inform classroom practice instead of one piece of data which doesn't help much. This approach will also help avoid cognitive overload because it is just two bits of data rather than several columns. I suppose what you can do with reading ages is then compare the reading age of the texts you share with your class and then decide if you are going to have to support reading or comprehending passages.

Cognitive Assessment Tests (CAT Tests) are used across many primary and secondary settings. There are four different sub-tests which then give schools a wealth of data. Scores from the four sub-tests are aggregated to give an average score. It is this average which in many cases is logged on marksheets and shared with staff. However, the average score alone doesn't tell you how well an individual performed in each of the sub-tests. The average score of 100 just tells you the individual scored within the broadly average range. However, they may have scored 80 in one sub-test and 120 in another, which tells you they actually have a relative strength in one area and another area which may need support. If we don't share this insight, then teaching staff are unlikely to adjust planning and their teaching to support the learner.

I fully appreciate that we need to be aware of cognitive overload for staff when sharing information and data, but are we rendering it less useful? We have spent time and money in gathering this data, so we have a responsibility to make best use of it. Part of your leadership therefore needs to be thinking about what staff need to know about data and how to adapt their teaching accordingly.

Your leadership could focus on using data scores from actual students to then explore how sub-test results might well impact on them accessing the curriculum. Supportive teaching approaches can then be discussed and put in place with a view to revisit them, their impact and next steps.

Avoid assumptions

Through my work with schools I have reviewed lots of data and talked through approaches to how it is used with senior leaders. In one school there was a bold claim that across their setting there was intelligent use of data. It then turned out through staff voice meetings that very few of the staff actually understood the data or the assessment scores that had been shared with them. As a leader, you are going to have to work on facts and not make any assumptions. A simple reflection from me is that throughout my four years of training to be a teacher, I was never once taught how to analyse and understand assessment data. I very much doubt this has changed over the years.

Identifying trends and changing needs

You may want to consider how you use data to give you and your staff a better understanding of needs at an individual, class and year level. If there are particular trends for specific classes or year groups, then you can identify these and share this information with teaching staff. You can help ensure that teaching is more targeted at meeting the needs of learners to support access and engagement. Effective analysis and interpretation of data can help suggest different strategies for staff to adopt based on the profile of needs within their class. Equally, if you know that there are particular barriers to learning or difficulties across a year group then you can adapt or adjust your targeted provision in order to support these learners to access the curriculum.

One year group is rarely the same as another year group, so you need to drill down and understand the differences. You need to assimilate information and process it so you can understand how staff might need to adapt their classroom approaches. Focus on the individual, classes and then whole year groups. This can help inform planning so that instead of having to react and adapt in the classroom, you can to some degree anticipate where difficulties may occur and then adjust how you intend to deliver specific content accordingly.

Tracking over time

What is happening over time? You can follow a class or a year group through the school and track their data to show how they have progressed over time. This might help highlight areas that teachers need to address in the classroom as there may be a high prevalence of the difficulty. This tracking over time might also highlight where particular reinforcement is needed in order to further develop particular skills.

This tracking over time can also be invaluable when it comes to transitions from year to year or from one setting to another. When you hand over from one member of staff to another you can focus in on key data so that staff can be fully prepared for the needs they are going to encounter. Again, planning and intended delivery can be adjusted beforehand to reduce the likelihood of staff struggling to meet needs during the first half term of the academic year as they get to know their class(es). You have this information so let's use it and avoid repeating cycles where some learners struggle at the start of the year because their teacher(s) don't understand their underlying needs.

This data you have can also influence how departments construct their curriculum or schemes of work. They can consider the underlying need of the cohort and plan for approaches that will help learners to engage with the subject. They can identify where learners may struggle with particular topics or how they are delivered and adapt them accordingly. Again, this is about making the assessment data work for staff to reduce the likelihood of issues arising later on. Considerations may include how vocabulary is introduced and reinforced, or how we scaffold for writing tasks so that learners are better able to fully demonstrate their knowledge and understanding.

I'm re-emphasising this point because you need to make sure that data informs actions and supports teaching staff in being able to understand how learners may engage in their lessons. You need to make sure that staff have everything they need so that they can use their professional training and insight to adapt their approaches and vary the strategies that they use within the classroom.

Using data to identify individuals who may need further support

We are going to look into this in more detail in a subsequent chapter but in short we can format our data to help identify learners who may struggle in a particular area. It can be as simple as conditionally formatting the data so you RAG (red, amber, green) rate it and identify learners who fall below a certain score in red or amber. Using your professional insight and knowledge you can start to understand how learners might experience difficulties in the classroom and wider learning environment. This knowledge can then support planning for further actions and, if necessary, additional assessments.

Don't be a crystal ball reader, involve the learners

There is a risk that when we have data, we use it solely to inform our understanding about an individual. We almost adopt a mystical approach where our interpretation of scores tells us exactly when and where a learner will experience difficulties. The truth is the data is a snapshot in time and only tells us part of the story. There needs to be some involvement with the individual themselves, so we get an understanding of where they feel they experience difficulties. We can then combine what we have to give a more holistic and comprehensive understanding of needs.

Sharing data with learners and families

There are some ethical considerations about sharing data with learners and their families, but you need to think about an opportunity to develop self-advocacy and consistency between home and school. Schools often share 'flight path' information, telling parents what the school believes their child will achieve if they continue to make progress at the same rate. How often then do you share data from other assessments, so they are aware of their child's overall development and profile? Perhaps there are opportunities to share key data so that parents are aware of it and can support their child accordingly. It might be an opportunity to ensure that there is greater consistency between home and school.

Rigour and reliability

Similar to the delivery of interventions there needs to be some consideration around the rigour and reliability of the data we have in our settings. If you are using standardised tests, then you need to make sure they are administered in the right conditions. You also need to make sure they are scored correctly. In some settings, assessments have been photocopied to reduce costs (breaking copyright), given to learners and then scored by staff. If staff have not had the correct training, then there may be some accuracy issues in the results. This then casts doubt over the final assessment scores and may render them less helpful in informing teaching approaches. In extreme cases you might have learners being placed on interventions because data suggests they need support in, for example, reading comprehension. That means one less place for another learner who might well actually need the support of the intervention.

Some reflection about rigour and reliability also boils down to scrutiny. If someone is going to be heavily scrutinised for poor scores, are they more likely to inflate them? If scores are for discussion to support teaching and learning decisions, then there may be more accuracy than if they are going to senior leaders who might question why learners have not made better progress.

Building a suite of assessments

Building on from our chapter which covered baselines, you can also consider how the assessments you have in your setting escalate from screening every learner to then screening groups or individuals we may have concerns about.

This is essentially applying the graduated approach to your assessments. If we focus in on cognition and learning for this example, you can list your assessments, which would fall into the following categories.

Universal: assessments used for every learner to provide an initial screening. This provides key data to support teaching and learning and gives an insight into any underlying issues. These could be reading assessments or cognitive ability tests.

Targeted: assessments that can be used if analysis of the universal assessment suggests there may be an underlying issue which needs further investigation. For reading, this might involve undertaking a comprehension assessment if initial scores suggest this is an area of weakness or that the standardised score from the universal assessment suggests the individual might benefit from access arrangements.

Specialist: assessments which are likely to be intensive and (relatively) time-consuming but which will give a really clear insight into, for example, specific areas such as decoding, comprehension and processing speeds. These are likely to be assessments that are recognised by the Joint Council for Qualifications so schools can apply for access arrangements for an individual.

If we look at an example model for cognition and learning assessments that go from Universal to Specialist, it may look something like this:

- **Universal** – New Group Reading Test, New Group Spelling Test, CAT

- **Targeted** – YARC (York Assessment of Reading Comprehension), Lucid Exact, Lucid Rapid

- **Specialist** – LASS, LADS, WRAT 5

There are plenty more assessments you could include for cognition and learning. You get the idea of how they can be used to escalate from initial screening to investigating concerns where scores suggest there may be an underlying issue. It is also worth considering which assessments meet JCQ (Joint Council for Qualifications) guidelines as they can be used as evidence when applying for access arrangements.

Another consideration for the targeted and specialist assessments is that to administer and/or score them, an individual needs a particular qualification. This may then feed back into your staff development plan; you can consider who in your team might want to develop their expertise around testing and access arrangements.

Why a graduated approach for assessments?

Think about time here. Assessments can be extremely time-consuming so you need to think about which assessments can be carried out that give useful data which you and your colleagues can effectively utilise. As you are screening whole cohorts you need something that is relatively easy to administer but which gives insightful data to support teaching approaches. Not every learner is going to require further investigation so this first screening needs to be effective in identifying who might need further screening and who doesn't.

If you were to use targeted or specialist assessments for whole cohort screening, then this is going to be extremely time-consuming. Consider the effort versus the effect and how much time has it taken to administer and score them and compare that to the impact the data has on classroom practices. Again, you have limited time and resources, so consider whether this intensive whole cohort screening is giving you value for money.

Targeted and specialist assessments are more time-consuming to administer and to score. You therefore need to be clear as to who needs further screening and be clear as to what you are going to do with the data. More importantly, what will teachers and the learner do with the data? How will both parties use it to inform strategies that they can adopt in the classroom (and beyond) to access text and key information?

Overall, your consideration here needs to be effort versus effect. How much time and cost goes into administering the assessments and what is the impact of the data that it provides. What is your department (and other departments/phases) doing with the data? How is that influencing approaches to teaching and learning in classrooms across the school?

Annual assessment schedule

To help plan out the year and manage your time and that of your team you may want to schedule when certain assessments are going to take place. Which assessments do you need to undertake in September with particular year groups to provide key data for the academic year?

Access arrangements are going to be a consideration so you can think about how you might structure your assessment schedule to reduce pressure across the year. It might be that for Year 9 you carry out a universal assessment in May or June; any student falling below a particular score can then be prioritised for targeted and specialist assessments. What this does is reduce the likelihood of having to react to concerns about learners needing access arrangements because you have screened the whole year group and have probably identified many of the learners who need additional considerations. There will still be some learners who will require additional testing, but they should be fewer in number. Think about how much time that may save you and your team in not having to respond to numerous concerns because the screening had not taken place before learners commenced GCSEs.

Reflection time

Are all staff aware of the assessment data made available to them? Do they access it?

_____
_____
_____
_____
_____
_____

Do all staff have an accurate understanding of the data and what it means for individuals and groups of learners?

_____
_____
_____
_____
_____
_____

How confident are you that assessments are administered properly to ensure rigour and reliability in the scores they are providing?

_____
_____
_____
_____
_____
_____

Which assessment might your school benefit from investing in to help guide overall teaching and learning practices?

_____
_____
_____
_____
_____
_____

Is assessment data used data to inform teaching and learning in every classroom? (Is this evident from conversations and learning walks?)

_____

_____

_____

_____

_____

_____

_____

From conversations with staff, are there any gaps in understanding data that need to be addressed through training? What actions do you need to take? Who can support or work with you on these actions?

_____

_____

_____

_____

_____

_____

_____

7 Training and services

SENCo as a consumer

One mindset to avoid is one where you, the SENCo, feels obliged to use certain services because that is what is on offer. In a free-market economy where academisation has radically changed the landscape, you need to avoid being a passive recipient of services, particularly but not limited to those supplied by the local authority (even if you are a maintained school). There may be a historical relationship in place but that doesn't mean you shouldn't be taking a step back to re-evaluate the quality of the services you are receiving. You need to ensure that in a dynamic world you are accessing the best possible support and guidance and using resources that will help with further developing inclusive approaches across your school.

Just like we have done in previous chapters, this is an opportunity to work out what your setting needs and who is best placed to deliver that service. At this point it is worth pointing out the need to be aware of key legislation like the Children and Families Act 2014, which then fed into the statutory guidance outlined in the SEND Code of Practice. I'm making reference to this because there are occasions where local authorities issue their own guidance to schools that is not actually linked to legislation. For instance, when seeking an education, health and needs assessment, some local authorities insist you use their staff before a request can be submitted. It might say something along the lines of using their specialist teachers before making a request, but you don't have to. What is good practice is to apply the graduated approach and use your best endeavours to better understand and then support the needs of an individual. If you use teachers or specialists outside of local authority employment, then that is your right if they are providing a high quality service.

Plotting where you need support

A good starting point is to reflect back on your own school context and work out where you feel support is most needed and where it will be most helpful.

It may be that you differentiate between support and training for staff and support for learners. Potentially you can create a list detailing what support would be helpful for universal practices, i.e. further developing inclusive classroom teaching. You can then identify what training and development your staff may need in order to further develop your additional provision / interventions across the school.

Your list might look like this.

Universal support – identifying training and development opportunities to support and further develop high-quality teaching. Working with teachers to understand possible barriers to learning and then sharing a range of strategies to support access and engagement. Using external specialists to undertake learning walks and review teaching and learning, offering guidance to further develop classroom practice. This might also include a reflection on resources that are given to learners and how they support access to and understanding of specific topics.

Targeted support – training to increase the offer of small group interventions across the school. Working with school staff to develop targeted interventions to meet learners' needs. Using external specialists to model small group work with learners to support staff confidence and competence in delivering interventions. This might also include buying 'off the shelf' programmes which come with training to support effective delivery.

Specialist support – intensive work with individual learners. Working with staff or learners to develop intensive 1:1 support programmes or undertake in-depth analysis of need for individual learners.

When you are developing your list, it might be worth considering where the biggest impact will be. There may well be occasions where it is necessary for specialists to work 1:1 with learners, but think about how often they work directly with all the school staff. If we can continuously improve the quality of teaching, then we can identify and address issues earlier. Needs will be better met in the classroom setting in the first instance, reducing the likelihood or need for additional provision. The reflections you undertook earlier in the provision section and where you identified areas for development can also feed into this scoping activity.

Undertaking research

Just sharing an anecdote here to reinforce my point. During lockdown both my dishwasher and oven broke. I then scoured the internet reading reviews from experts and customers, checking prices in a bid to find reliable, high-quality replacements. The other challenge was making sure they would do what I needed them to do, would fit in the space I had and that they were energy efficient. Eventually, I managed to buy two products that are working well today, so the research and attention to detail paid off. The question is, do we invest this much time into researching the services or products that will help our setting be more inclusive? How confident are you that you are getting the best possible deal and that your schools are receiving the highest quality service that represents good value for money? It is worth pointing out here that even 'free' training and support has a cost attached to it – the cost of time, the potential to put your staff off engaging with training in the future – so it is important to research them thoroughly beforehand.

Every local authority will have a local offer (some are better than others) so this might be a good starting point to look for services that will support you in your work. You also have SENCo networks and forums that provide the opportunity to gain insight from colleagues into their experience of working with particular agencies and services. You might like to know how flexible the service providers are, how prompt they are in returning communication or supplying reports. All of this can feed into your decision-making.

Check with existing customers

Whether it is training or goods you are looking to purchase you should be able to check with existing customers. This will help you get an insight into just how good the training or product actually is. You may also be able to learn from the experiences of others so that you avoid any errors they may have made along the way. It might also be prudent to check whether any existing customer making an endorsement gets a referral fee. You really need to make sure that any views shared are impartial and reflect the actual experience other customers have been through.

This is also an opportunity to find out the reality behind the claims. In a commercial world there are some confident claims behind the impact of training or products sold by companies. By speaking to existing customers, you will hopefully get the cold, hard truth and a clearer understanding behind the actual impact you are likely to gain.

You deciding what you want

It is at this point that, in addition to the services you would like, you can also start to think about the manner in which they are delivered. You know the needs and the context of your setting so you are best placed to outline how you feel a service should be delivered. Just like the 'if it ain't broke' statement, you may need to re-evaluate how services are provided in your setting. You are the consumer, so you have the right to say what you want, what you need and how you think it should be delivered.

Challenge tradition: don't be dictated to by visiting professionals or services delivering in a way they have got comfortable with. If your context has changed, then it is perfectly acceptable to request the manner in which services or support you receive adapt and evolve with your setting. Just like your provision in school what you are receiving should be demand-led and not supply-led. Support needs to be based around your school needs.

Make them earn their money

In terms of visiting professionals working with learners it is worth considering how you are getting the most out of them, their time and their expertise. I think it is the job of SENCos to really challenge visiting professionals and services. The more you apply the graduated approach, the more you consider needs and do your utmost to support them, then the more challenge you are presenting to visiting professionals. What you then need is advice and guidance over and above what you have already done.

This comes back to challenging the status quo and not just accepting how professionals have traditionally delivered their service or support. The last thing you want or need is for someone to come in and give you obvious, basic strategies. You need to ensure you have already put those in place, reviewed them and then done more. Essentially, if you are being visited by specialists you need them to be challenged. They are after all the 'big guns', so you need them to tell you something you don't already know. If they can't add to what you have put in place, then you might just have to look elsewhere for support that does build on your robust practices.

Agreeing expected outcomes

Really, the same principles apply for training and support; we need to think about what it is we want and what success will look like. We can't afford to be passive recipients – there is too much at stake. There has to be a focus on establishing clear criteria so we know what to expect and what our professionals will be providing or delivering. Just like our vision, if we have clear outcomes in place from the outset then we can revisit them if we feel we have deviated from them.

Some questions to consider:

- How will this training or support help with the development needs of the staff or needs of our learners across our setting?
- Are we able to plan out how support or training will be delivered across the academic year?
- Can we work together to agree what the success criteria will be?
- What evidence and research are you able to cite to support the content and design of the training or support?
- How has the content been accredited or quality assured?
- Can we do a run through of the training before it is delivered to the staff?
- Are you able to provide a breakdown of your costs to show the ratio between planning and delivery?
- What training and qualifications do your staff have in delivering training or support in schools?
- How will we know the training or support has made a difference? What are your methods for evaluation?
- Is there additional reading available to help further support staff development if they are interested in the training topic?
- What follow-up training or support will take place to embed guidance that has been shared?

The list of questions is not exhaustive, you can probably add plenty more, but they are the start of a dialogue. They can help ensure you get what you want and need from professionals and service providers. It is an opportunity for there to be absolute clarity in what you need and what you will then receive. The clearer we are from the outset then the more we can challenge when things are not being delivered as agreed.

Try before you buy!

If we are considering training for our staff, then we really need to be confident about what it is we are going to be receiving. Again, even if it is free, there is still a cost involved. Staff training time is extremely valuable, so we need to make the most of it.

It is perfectly acceptable to ask to see any training materials and get the provider to walk through what the session will look like and how it will advance understanding around a topic or theme. I would suggest going as far as checking content and layout of training slides so you can gauge whether they reflect good practice. Equally, the style of delivery can be discussed. This is training for adults not children. We need to consider andragogical approaches rather than pedagogical approaches. Andragogy focuses in on how adults learn rather than pedagogical approaches used in the classroom with young learners. How will the trainers engage your staff so that they build on prior experience, capitalise on self-concepts and motivation to learn?

You could even get the trainer to give you a 10-minute taster so you can get a feel of their delivery style. This is important because if you are leading new approaches to special educational needs across your setting, you need staff to come with you and not be turned off by a dull presenter. The best training is going to challenge thinking by getting staff talking about content and reflecting on their own practice and then identifying actions which they will actually focus on after the training. Someone reading slide after slide is unlikely to get that buy-in or enthusiasm and commitment from staff so it is definitely worth reviewing training before you commit to it.

Don't think this is a cheeky request asking someone to go through their training with you – it is far from it. You have a responsibility to your school community to make sure you secure high-quality training. Finding out after the session that they are not particularly as good as they made out is way too late. Do your due diligence beforehand to make sure this individual deserves a starring role in front of your colleagues.

Does it represent value for money?

Our research should also involve a focus on the cost of receiving the training or support. It is perfectly reasonable to receive a breakdown of any fees or charges you are going to have to pay. You can then decide if they are reasonable. For instance, you may want to review the ratio of preparation time to delivery time to see if this is reasonable. Are you being charged preparation time for something that already exists and only needs minor amendments? It may be that you are being charged a full day for a half day of training because the provider is unable to engage in other work that day. Again, it is down to you to decide what is reasonable and what is perhaps more costly than it needs to be.

Your research may also involve the creation of a table where you can compare and contrast what is on offer from different providers. The table can compare expected outcomes, pros and cons of each provider and a cost. Whilst there will always be budgetary implications, the better the support you access then the better you are serving your whole school community.

Join forces with another school

If costs do appear to be onerous then it might be an idea to communicate with other schools to see if you can have a joint training event. You have the potential to agree a focus and then share the overall costs between different schools making it more affordable to run training sessions.

The other bonus of taking this approach is that you can encourage staff at different schools to work collaboratively and share their knowledge, expertise and learning with one another. You help staff see opportunities to teaching beyond their own setting and explore approaches that might help improve their classroom practice.

In terms of services, if there is a specific type of training that is particularly hard to access then it might be an opportunity for schools to pool resources and employ a professional themselves. An example of this might be an educational psychologist: we know they are a scarce resource and aren't always able to make it into schools as often as we would hope. If schools jointly employ an educational psychologist, then you can get more regular access to them and also establish how you want them to work in your setting so you get the most out of the relationship.

Making it stick

One of the final considerations for training is exploring how it will become embedded across your school. We know from research that one-off training events are less effective at changing behaviour or practices. What is needed is a plan for how training or support will be delivered and then exploring and identifying opportunities for it to be revisited across the year. We need to consider creating a framework so learning can be assimilated, put into practice and then for staff to come back and collaborate about their experiences (we call it retrieval practice when we are working with young people but don't always apply the same practice with adults). Revisiting training can support reflection and the sharing of learning, leading to further experimentation and development of inclusive practices in your setting.

Quality over quantity has to be a consideration if we are going to make new ideas and ways of working stick. This comes directly from my work undertaking SEND reviews in schools. During staff voice meetings, there were positive comments about the amount of training received but questions were raised about the quantity. Some settings had chosen to cover lots of areas of SEND such as dyslexia, ADHD, autism, dyspraxia and so on. Whilst staff appreciated training opportunities, there were some frustrations around not being able to revisit topics to share learning. A leadership action for you as a SENCo is going to be around working out what your priority is and then focusing on that.

Consider training and development over the course of an academic year. Remember a one-off jazz hands session, whilst engaging and possibly entertaining, is unlikely to change practices. Consider what complementary activities you can plan across the academic year so that staff revisit training, take on further theory and then set themselves a goal to further improve their practice. It may be helpful to get staff to commit to one change; if there are any more than that they might not receive the attention they should. What we want is for staff to think differently to improve their overall practice and to have sustainable and sustained improvements.

An example of how you might revisit training is where you initially focus on high-quality teaching. In the training you agree with staff a definition for high-quality teaching, explore possible barriers learners may experience, different teaching strategies and how they can be used over time to support learners. The revisit part could involve staff thinking about a learner in their class, exploring their barriers to learning and then thinking about the strategies that might help the learner access work in lessons. Staff then go off and put this plan into action, observing and noting what works and what might be less effective. A subsequent training session will then focus on sharing these actions. You can ask: What did we learn? What did we struggle with? How did the learner respond? What are future areas for development? This can also be a platform to share and celebrate good practice.

Reflection time

What are the key areas in which you need further training, development and resources?

_____

_____

_____

_____

_____

_____

_____

What actions will you take in locating high-quality support and guidance? Who can help signpost you to high-quality providers?

_____

_____

_____

_____

_____

_____

_____

Start to outline the expected outcomes you need from training and services so you can refine them with colleagues later.

_____

_____

_____

_____

_____

_____

_____

What are the key features of high-quality support that you will need from professionals working with your school? Can you share these beforehand to vet potential suppliers?

_____

_____

_____

_____

_____

_____

_____

Outline steps you can use in a vetting process to make sure you only work with quality providers.

_____

_____

_____

_____

_____

_____

_____

How can colleagues work with you to ensure that training, support or guidance is embedded into staff practice?

_____

_____

_____

_____

_____

_____

_____

8 High-quality teaching

High-quality teaching analogy

Imagine standing in front of a very large dam which is starting to spring leaks in various places. You stand in one place working out how to plug that leak when a different one appears in another part of the dam. You could spend all your time plugging the leaks, tirelessly working to make sure every gap in the dam is plugged. Despite all your efforts, they keep on springing up. Alternatively, you could make sure that the dam is built properly in the first place and is robust in its nature. Leaks may well appear, but they will be fewer in number. And that is my analogy about high-quality teaching.

The more we get it right in the classroom, the less likely it is that learners will need to leave for additional support and interventions. Some learners may need to go out for specific support but if we get high-quality teaching right then more can remain in the classroom because the pedagogical diet is better for them. Their needs are being met through teaching staff being able to use a repertoire of strategies that support access to the curriculum.

Below, I will go through some quotes from the SEND Code of Practice to highlight why understanding what we mean by high-quality teaching and being able to articulate what it looks like within the classroom is essential. The focus here is on the teacher and in them being able to use a variety of strategies and being able to differentiate approaches for individuals. There is also the need to highlight that it is the teacher's responsibility in the first instance to make adjustments to their practice in order to support learners to access the curriculum. Before any referrals are made, we need to know which actions and reasonable adjustments have been made by the class teacher.

Exploring what the SEND Code of Practice says about teaching

It is worth starting with the SEND Code of Practice as there are several statements which highlight the importance of high-quality teaching. I am using the statements to act as a reference rather than in a finger-wagging manner to tell teachers they need to get it right in the classroom (!). The other reason for using the statements is to reinforce the loose use of language in education and how the lack of clarity can be costly when moving forward with planning, training and development.

I have chosen quotes from Chapters 1 and 6 of the Code of Practice, which contain statements on high-quality teaching. I've used bold on keywords to highlight a key consideration for you as a SENCo later on.

> *1.24 **High quality teaching** that is **differentiated and personalised** will meet the individual needs of the majority of children and young people. Some children and young people need educational provision that is additional to or different from this. This is special educational provision under Section 21 of the Children and Families Act 2014. Schools and colleges must use their best endeavours to ensure that such provision is made for those who need it. Special educational provision is underpinned by **high quality teaching** and is compromised by anything less.*

> *6.15 A pupil has SEN where their learning difficulty or disability calls for special educational provision, namely provision different from or additional to that normally available to pupils of the same age. Making higher quality teaching normally available to the whole class is likely to mean that fewer pupils will require such support. Such improvements in whole-class provision tend to be more cost effective and sustainable.*

> *6.19 The first response to such progress should be **high quality teaching** targeted at their areas of weakness. Where progress continues to be less than expected the class or subject teacher, working with the SENCO, should assess whether the child has SEN. While informally gathering evidence (including the views of the pupil and their parents) schools should not delay in putting in place extra teaching or other rigorous interventions designed to secure better progress, where required. The pupil's response to such support can help identify their particular needs.*

> *6.37 **High quality teaching**, **differentiated for individual pupils**, is the first step in responding to pupils who have or may have SEN. Additional intervention and support cannot compensate for a lack of good quality teaching. Schools should regularly and carefully review the quality of teaching for all pupils, including those at risk of underachievement. This includes reviewing and, where necessary, improving, teachers' understanding of strategies to identify and support vulnerable pupils and their knowledge of the SEN most frequently encountered.*

So, in all, across the SEND Code of Practice there are six references to high-quality teaching; I've quoted four of them. One reflection I would encourage you to take is, having read the above four statements, are you clear as to what high-quality teaching is and what it involves in the classroom? Do we have clear definitions or a lot of sound bites that sound virtuous but do little to understand what great teaching actually involves?

Language matters

Language really does matter, not just in terms of developing positive approaches and attitudes to inclusion but in establishing clear starting points from which to progress from. I would argue that, although high-quality teaching is referenced in the code of practice six times, it is not defined at all. I have seen several presentations where experts use some of the statements featured above as ways of defining what high-quality teaching is, but they simply don't.

Let's unpick 6.37 as an example. OK, we start off with '**High quality teaching, differentiated for individual pupils'**. No mention of what high-quality teaching actually is, it is just used as statement, almost a matter of fact that we should all know what it is and what it involves. This is then followed by '**differentiated for individual pupils'**; differentiation, the much maligned, misinterpreted and misquoted term in education. Differentiation, in my opinion, means everything and nothing at the same time. It is a term thrown around far too readily when you pose the question 'How do you meet the needs of the learners?'. Bang, 'differentiation', the one-word panacea that fixes all difficulties in the classroom.

The point (rather than the rant) is that we use certain terms in education, but we don't always define them clearly. We hear a certain term, and we all nod our heads indicating we know what is being talked about, but is that the reality? Is my understanding of differentiation the same as yours? The risk is that if we do not have a concrete and consistent understanding of key terms, in particular high-quality teaching, then when we progress, we risk staff going off on tangents. The lack of absolute clarity may mean that there is inconsistency across the whole school because individuals and departments have their own nuanced understanding of what they feel high-quality teaching is and how it should be delivered in the classroom. This inconsistency may then mean you find yourself with an extremely leaky dam and high demand for interventions

Are we all on the same page?

A good starting point is to work with all staff in your setting to explore their understanding of high-quality teaching. How would they define it? What would it look like in each classroom? This gives you a good starting point because you are establishing where all your staff are at. This is your foundation from which to build on. It means you have clarity and are not progressing on assumptions.

Getting staff to give a definition for high-quality teaching is a simple, low-stakes activity, but it gives you so much information. Do the staff actually have a secure understanding of what great pedagogy involves? Anything that is not a clear definition of high-quality teaching can then alert you to addressing misconceptions for the whole staff or identifying individuals who may need more support and training in the future.

Once we have a clear definition and understanding of high-quality teaching, we can think about how we can further develop the term and therefore continue to evolve inclusive classroom practices. The important thing is that this is not high-quality teaching for learners with SEND, this is high-quality teaching for every learner. By taking this approach we avoid any 'bolt-ons' where some staff may feel reluctant to use certain approaches. This is about meeting the needs of all learners, ensuring access and engagement through our teaching.

There are some great resources out there to support any training with staff on exploring what high-quality teaching is and what it involves. Some of the resources I recommend in my role supporting schools include:

- What Makes Great Teaching? – Sutton Trust
- Developing Great Teaching – Teacher Development Trust
- Effective Teaching – Education Development Trust
- Personalised Learning: A Practical Guide – DCSF
- Principles of Instruction – Rosenshine

There are plenty of resources and lots of research which you can draw on to start your planning for training on high-quality teaching. I would argue that for your setting, you need to come up with your own definition. Given your unique context, what do you feel high-quality teaching is, involves and looks like? This ultimately is going to be inextricably linked to your vision. Why is high-quality teaching important? Well, if we get it right, we improve the life chances and opportunities for future generations.

Leaders working together with one message

There is likely to be a lead in your setting who oversees teaching and learning or learning and teaching depending on your viewpoint. This person has to be someone you work closely with so that there is one clear consistent message around high-quality teaching. It can't be that they stand up and talk about great classroom practice and then hand over to you so you can talk about what to do if learners have SEND. It has to be 'this is what we do to meet the needs of learners in our setting'. It really has to be a case of this is good practice for all.

It would be worth arranging time with them to go through proposals for further developing high-quality teaching in your setting. More importantly, this is an opportunity to establish whether you are on the same page or whether you have fundamental differences in how you interpret and define high-quality teaching. You need to ensure that you reach a point where you both agree on what great teaching involves and looks like across the school.

Trust is important, agreement is not

In some respects, if you don't initially agree then this is a good starting point. Having someone whom you trust but disagree with will help sharpen your thinking. How secure are you with your understanding of high-quality teaching – and in your ability to share it with other staff? If you can't explain it coherently to one person, how are you going to convince 20+ people that it is paramount they get it right? This discussion and disagreement is a great opportunity to help you sharpen your thinking so you have better clarity and confidence in an area you are likely to receive some direct questioning on.

This challenge will also help you avoid the head-nodding with your teaching and learning lead only to find out at a later point in time that you were nodding heads with a different understanding. You need to ensure you are on the same page and that you can partner one another in a complementary way to further establish a clear understanding of high-quality teaching in your setting.

Barriers to accessing and engaging with learning

Before we look at strategies that staff might use to support learners, it is worth firstly exploring the barriers. Given that we have already covered that you work in a unique setting, then it is worth establishing with the staff what they feel may be barriers for learners in your school (or in their classes).

This provides an invaluable insight into what the teachers feel are the barriers to learning compared to what you know the barriers are. Regardless, it provides a starting point for discussions and perhaps an opportunity for you to address any misconceptions certain staff may have.

It might also be helpful to focus on the strengths of the learners being taught by each teacher. What can learners do well, this might be an opportunity to build on strengths rather than focusing solely on deficits.

What strategies do we use?

Once you come up with a commonly agreed definition for high-quality teaching in your setting and then established barriers to learning it might then be helpful to explore teaching strategies. What approaches and strategies can staff adopt in order to support access and engagement in their lessons? This is almost a 'so what?' opportunity after you have established the barriers. If you know these are some of the barriers which impact on learners, then ask yourself what is being about them.

There are at least two ways you can approach discussing and sharing inclusive classroom strategies.

The first approach might involve you sharing lists of different strategies that staff can use, having them on slides and then sharing them with staff. This gives you the opportunity to share what you know to be good practice in supporting learners. Staff can then refer back to these lists in the event of them having difficulty supporting a learner.

The second approach can involve staff having the barriers to learning in front of them and then listing the strategies they use to support access and engagement. Different approach, no better or worse but it does give you another opportunity to gain an insight into what staff know about inclusive practice. Anything they write down can be collated and typed up into a list which is then shared across the whole staff. This then combines with your high-quality teaching definition to form your whole school approach to inclusive practice in the classroom.

If you go with the second approach, then you can look out for strategies staff said they use when you carry out your learning walks. Do staff adopt the strategies they talk about or is this a leadership action for you to remind and then mentor or coach staff in adopting the strategies that you all agreed will help support learners.

Don't forget your Ordinarily Available Provision

When you are developing your in-house strategies, you also have the opportunity of using any that your local authority might have shared as part of their drive to support universal approaches in schools. It might be worthwhile chunking these so that they are more accessible and easier to process for staff. This will also help embed the language we hope that staff use when they communicate what they have done to support learners in the classroom.

Using the OAP strategies is also an opportunity to support any referrals by outlining what you have adopted from the LA's list plus additional ones you have developed as a school. Again, this is all about reinforcing that the classroom is the first line of intervention. It might also be the case to highlight that your setting uses strategies not listed by your LA. An opportunity to highlight inclusive practices and to reiterate your expectation that visiting specialists need to provide you with insightful strategies you have not yet considered or implemented.

Reinforce and build on the strategies

Whatever strategies you share or develop with staff are going to be your starting point. Thinking about cognitive load for staff, there is no way you can share hundreds of strategies in one session with staff and expect them to retain them. Just like with learners in the classroom, chunk what you want to share. Ensure that teaching staff have clarity on how they would adopt each strategy.

Once we have confidence that the initial strategies are being used in the right way then we can revisit them in future sessions. It is a great opportunity to support staff collaboration and discussion in how they adopted and implemented different strategies in their classroom. I know there is a big focus (quite rightly) on evidence informed practice, but we need to take an approach of; evidence informed, practice refined. Some strategies take a while to master so we may need to persevere. It doesn't mean the strategies aren't effective, it is more the case we have to get better at knowing when and how to use them. These staff discussions and potential collaborations provide an ideal opportunity to support staff reflection and future development.

If we take this approach of revisiting, reflecting, discussing, collaborating and sharing good practice we can see that high-quality teaching becomes more of a dynamic entity. We haven't just said 'this is high-quality teaching, get on with it'. We have created an environment where if a learner is struggling, we hope the initial reflection will be 'What can I do differently?' rather than the teacher blaming the learner for not understanding.

Move beyond condition-specific approaches

Just as we have outlined that learners are getting more complex, we need to be mindful of compartmentalising strategies to specific learning differences. Just because a learner may have a diagnosis doesn't necessarily mean that all the strategies linked to it will work. For example, strategies listed for a learner with autism will not all work, and some may work for a learner who has not been diagnosed with autism. We need staff to understand the actual needs the individual has and then consider what can be done to best support them.

High-quality teaching strategies don't just support the learners

As we build strategies staff can draw upon, we build confidence amongst our staff. This is far more important than we might initially think. From visits to schools the message being communicated over and over is that learners' needs are getting more complex. The challenges experienced in the classroom are far greater. We need to acknowledge that increased challenge without increased training is likely to lead to anxiety. What we did before no longer seems to have the same, effective impact as it once had. That is a tough message for classroom practitioners to hear.

Ensuring that high-quality teaching is seen as dynamic and ever-evolving hopefully creates a climate of reflection. If needs are evolving and getting more complex then so must our approaches and the strategies we use. Complex difficulties are likely to require complex solutions. The more strategies we are able to draw on then the more confidence we have in being able to adapt our approach in order to engage our learners.

Heuristic not formulaic

Whilst I fully appreciate the role of training and mentoring, I feel quite strongly that teaching is heuristic. Heuristic involves learning and discovery through experimentation, evaluating practices and some trial and error. Becoming a good teacher involves more than completing a course, reading a book or following a lesson plan, it involves deep reflection and an ongoing understanding what works, along with the conditions that make approaches more or less effective. This reflection helps individuals to flex and adapt in the classroom in light of the experience they have gained and assimilated to inform their own practice.

To this end simply supplying someone with a list of strategies is not going to improve their practice. We need to create the right conditions where individuals feel they can take responsibility for their own practice. Think of it along the lines of growth mindset. The best teachers are going to be the ones that take the greatest risks, make the most mistakes but get up, dust themselves down and continue to improve and evolve what they are doing in the classroom. This has to be celebrated as part of the ongoing journey towards great teaching.

When we are leading on high-quality teaching, we therefore need to ensure it is not seen as a formula to follow. It is an experiment; we are likely to make mistakes, but they present us with learning opportunities. How often do we tell children to learn from their mistakes but play it so safely in the classroom that we don't make any? The leadership of high-quality teaching therefore needs to be supportive, encouraging and non-judgemental. We need to be curious about classroom practices and learning and think about where the lesson is going and how learners are progressing. If there are capability issues, then we deal with those on an individual basis but on a whole school level we want to support ongoing development.

SEND Policy and Teaching and Learning Policy

The last point to consider when moving forward is that once you have a clear outline and definition for high-quality teaching it is making sure that there is just one definition across all policies. Having done all the legwork and collaboration with senior colleagues and staff it really is ensuring that one definition is used in the SEND Policy and the school's Teaching and Learning Policy. They have to be the same, verbatim, great high-quality teaching is great high-quality teaching.

A leadership action you can take is working with the teaching and learning lead to review the Teaching and Learning Policy. Is it still fit for purpose and how does it align with the school's own vision for supporting learners to achieve great outcomes? This could be an opportunity to re-define high-quality teaching and amend any associated guidance so that staff are clear as to their role inside and outside the classroom.

High-quality teaching

I am well aware that I have talked about high-quality teaching and have been critical where it has not been clearly defined whilst going through a whole chapter without definining it myself. So, here goes with my definition. I believe high-quality teaching is where staff understand the barriers to engagement experienced by learners, and are able to draw on and use a variety of strategies to support and engage learners. Learners develop skills and knowledge which helps them build confidence and independence over time. I would probably also add that high-quality teaching has an element of being context based, as different learners will need different approaches to support access and engagement with the curriculum.

Reflection time

What is your definition of high-quality teaching?

_____

_____

_____

_____

_____

_____

_____

What is the definition of high-quality teaching shared by your teaching and learning lead?

_____
_____
_____
_____
_____
_____

Does your SEND Policy define high-quality teaching? Does that match the definition in the school's Teaching and Learning Policy?

_____
_____
_____
_____
_____
_____

What are some of the things you would expect to see if high-quality teaching was taking place in a classroom?

_____
_____
_____
_____
_____
_____

Which members of staff could be your champions for leading on high-quality teaching?

_____
_____
_____
_____
_____
_____

Consider some non-negotiables you might share with staff that need to be in place for high-quality teaching to be effective.

_____
_____
_____
_____
_____
_____
_____

What are your next steps in further promoting high-quality teaching across your setting?

_____
_____
_____
_____
_____
_____
_____

9 The role of the teaching assistant

The role of the TA

For the sake of this book, I am using TA, as in teaching assistant, to cover all the different names used to describe or label adults who provide support to learners inside of lessons. Here are some other terms that are used:

INA   Individual Needs Assistant
CSA   Classroom Support Assistant
SNA   Special Needs Assistant
SSA   Special Support Assistant
TA   Teaching Assistant
LSA   Learning Support Assistant
PC   Progress Coach
LC   Learning Coach
LM   Learning Mentor

Feel free to add in your own acronyms (you can then play acronym bingo to see if anyone understands what each one refers to!).

I think if you are arguing over whether someone is an LSA, TSA or CSA then you are missing the point. The real challenge is being clear on how we need them to operate across the learning environment in order to have the most impact. From my perspective, this is not about job titles, it is about exploring the role of support in lessons which I feel is extremely complex in its nature. Let's get the support right first and then we can discuss titles later.

What the research tells us

Teaching assistants are not a new phenomenon, they have been supporting in schools for decades, but essentially the same challenge remains. What support and guidance do we need to give to teaching assistants in order for them to understand how to carry out their role to maximise the impact of their presence? How is that information also shared with teachers so they can make best use of additional adults in their classrooms?

We have plenty of research and resources to draw upon to give us a starting point:

- Teaching reforms and the impact of paid adult support on participation and learning in mainstream schools 2003
- Deployment and Impact of Support Staff 2009
- Effective deployment of support staff – TDA 2010
- TA Deployment review guide – London Leadership Strategy
- Making Best Use of TAs 2015
- Making sense of 'teaching', 'support' and 'differentiation': the educational experiences of pupils with Education, Health and Care Plans and Statements in mainstream secondary schools 2018

Early evidence suggested that the main focus from support staff was on task completion instead of focusing on the learning. This is totally understandable though, consider the following question: How do you know your TA has been effective in your lesson? Is there a perception that TAs are there to ensure that learners get on and complete their work? Whether this is reality or not you can imagine that some TAs feel that they need to get learners to do their work and answer questions in order to demonstrate how invaluable they are as a TA, because there doesn't otherwise seem to be an obvious way to prove they are having an effect. It is useful to explore and consider the responses from teaching staff and from TAs in order to assess whether this is the case in your school.

In short, what we know is that the more support learners receive the less progress they make over time. So, you need to bear this in mind when considering the role of the TA in your setting. This was borne out of the research from the Deployment and Impact of Support Staff. Research gathered from the project showed that the more support pupils received from teaching assistants, the less academic progress they made. From my perspective, support was perhaps more focused on getting the work done rather than focusing on how to support individuals to learn what was being taught in the lesson. This focus on task completion perhaps then created a dependency whereby learners felt unable to tackle tasks without the presence of a TA.

Gather your own evidence base

To help support any planning for the future, it would be helpful to undertake research of your own. Through learning walks, lesson observations and talking to other staff who undertake learning walks or lesson drop-ins, assess and evaluate what practices you are seeing from the TAs working in your setting. This is an opportunity for you to gain a baseline and an understanding of where your starting point is, which can then help inform any actions you will need to take when moving forward.

You can use the review guide above or RAG rate what you feel are key characteristics of effective support. This will give you an indication of the amount of training you may have to undertake or put in place for your TAs to get them from where they are to the ideal TA role.

Link to your vision

If we go back to our SEND vision, what do we ultimately want to achieve for our learners? If we believe that our ultimate goal is ensuring that our learners are able to engage and contribute to wider society with growing independence once they leave our setting, then we need to factor this into our thinking. This links in with preparation for adulthood; we are not just supporting a unit of data, we are supporting a human being who needs to be ready for the challenges that will be presented to them in their next stage of education, employment, training and life when they leave us.

Start with the role

If we link back to every setting being unique, then you need to think about how you want TAs to operate and function within your own school context. Just because you employ a TA from another setting who comes with glowing references, does not necessarily mean they are going to be effective in yours.

An essential starting point is working with TAs to explore and clarify the role in your setting. What are the key features of effective support in your setting? What are the different approaches and strategies that TAs can adopt in order to support, whilst also developing independence over time? It is important to work with your TA team to explore this role because ultimately, they are going to have to own it and undertake that role every working day. This is very much a case of walking alongside your staff and joining them on their journey rather than you writing the role and walking ahead whilst they might be struggling behind you because they don't know how to undertake the role you have written in isolation.

The early research is quite damning but is potentially a sobering reminder that support gone wrong disempowers and creates dependency rather than independence. Effective support is like effective leadership: things continue to function well when you are not around!

So, I need to do myself out of a job?

It is worth reflecting on the ultimate role of the TA when progressing with an outline of how they will operate. The cold, hard truth is that if a TA is effective then the learner(s) they are working with becomes independent and no longer needs their support. Effectively, because they have been so great in their role then they are no longer needed. That is quite a tough reality. Of course, there are likely to be other learners who need support, but it is a difficult predicament to find yourself in.

It may then be helpful to move beyond the sometimes binary nature of SEND provision. There will be times when learners with SEND need support and times when they don't. Equally, just because a learner has not been identified with SEND doesn't mean that they don't experience difficulties in lessons and may benefit from support. This is about supporting learning in the classroom, not just focusing on those identified as learners with SEND.

Develop a mission statement

This is a great opportunity to come up with a statement that is more focused than a job description or a list of bullet points outlining the role of a TA (although this is useful as well). Think of a mission statement as your intent, your battle cry for TAs. This is going to clearly but succinctly outline what the overall purpose of having TAs in the learning environment is.

Through your work with your TA team and building on research you may come up with a simple statement clearly indicating the whole purpose of TA support in the classroom. This may include the aim of supporting ongoing independence, partnering with teaching staff and sharing feedback on who was engaged, who struggled and at which point difficulties appeared to occur.

Again, I think it is important to work with your team because they have to commit to the mission. If we are going to create something that clearly outlines our intent, then we need to make sure everyone is onboard. In some respects, this is our offer, almost an advertisement — this is what TAs are going to do in the classroom in order to deliver effective support and develop independent and confident learners.

Once we have our mission statement then we can share it across the school. Just like our vision, we can come back to it to reinforce approaches to support. It helps us to highlight the importance of supporting independence. When challenged with 'Why are we doing this?', you have your mission statement to act as your consistent anchor. This is our goal, this is our mission, this is why we need to develop in this direction. We are developing independence over time which may mean that we support less to help learners think and act for themselves. It doesn't mean support is not there, it just means from time to time we have to let individuals learn how to struggle so they can work some things out for themselves.

Train all staff in understanding the role

This comes from my experience of delivering training across a range of schools. We can train and develop our TAs so they have a clear understanding of what great support looks like and involves. They have the opportunity to become proficient TAs in the classrooms they are deployed to. They know about developing independence, they observe, they listen and they wait for the right time to intervene. However, if training has not been shared beyond the TAs, then the class teacher may then direct the TA to work with an individual or group of learners and talks about helping them. 'Help' is probably interpreted in several different ways between the teacher and TA. Instead of being empowered to survey the class and target where support is needed, the TA is directed to perhaps work with individuals to make sure the work gets done. This means the TA doesn't necessarily develop independence and there is little scope for them to circulate the classroom because they have been given a role for that lesson.

To help avoid your well-trained TA workforce being deployed in the wrong way or not being able to use their skills effectively, then training all staff in understanding the role of a TA is essential. Teaching staff need to understand the approaches TAs may well take. For example, they need to understand the self-scaffolding framework which features under recommendation 3 of the *Making Best Use of Teaching Assistants Guidance Report*. The framework is great in highlighting the approaches that teaching assistants can take in order to develop learner independence over time. The premise is that we want learners to think through tasks before intervening or offering support. They need time to think through their challenge and to try to work out for themselves what they need to do to progress. The onus is on the individual to think, the teaching assistant can stand back and look to see how the individual is progressing and observe at what points difficulties might occur. The model has several layers:

- self-scaffolding
- prompting
- clueing
- modelling
- correcting.

If it looks like learners are unable to self-scaffold then a TA might prompt, then clue, then model until they reach the bottom of the framework. The last option is correcting; this is where answers are given, and it requires no independent thinking from the learners. So, the overall aim is to let learners think, get them to consider and then respond to the challenge and avoid creating a dependency culture where TAs do all the work and learners do little if any at all.

Once all staff are aware of the role TAs can undertake in supporting across the learning environment then it can help with effective deployment. If you know that a TA is going to observe and look for the point at which learners begin to struggle, then you are going to want to know that information, so it feeds into your understanding of the class. What can you do differently when planning and delivering your lesson so that more learners are engaged? Equally, how can you adapt your planning so that you empower the TA and get maximum benefit from their presence?

Gather more evidence

Introducing and highlighting the role of TAs is going to take more than one staff training session or meeting. A leadership action is then going to involve undertaking learning walks and observing consistency across different classrooms. It is an opportunity to be curious and wonder just how well different staff work together and the level of empowerment afforded to your TAs.

Your curiosity-driven information-gathering can then help you gain an insight into the consistency of practices across your setting. Which members of teaching staff work really well with TAs? Which ones need further support to gain maximum benefit from a TA's presence in their classroom?

You may need to speak with individual teachers to explore and understand what some of the barriers are to effective TA deployment. This information can then support future staff training because you can share the barriers and then share how other members of staff overcame these same barriers. Better still, you can use teaching staff to share their own experiences, so colleagues get a clear insight into the actions others have taken. This might be more of an effective approach as opposed to you, the leader for the TAs (i.e. someone with a vested interest), telling teaching staff about successful strategies to overcome barriers.

Revisit the role, share, collaborate and listen

In leading your TA team you have the opportunity to revisit and discuss how the role is progressing across your setting. Team meetings can periodically be dedicated to discussing how support in classrooms is progressing with an honest focus on challenges alongside success. From your learning walks you can also share what your curiosity led you to consider about support practices.

The mission statement can be revisited, gauging how well the team is doing and the progress being made towards consistently delivering effective support across the setting. This is a journey we are on; it may take some time but working as a team, being honest and open can help in making progress and improving support practices.

Your listening as a leader will also help in you planning future support and training for your TA team. Your training can be more targeted to meet the needs and the stages of development across your team. It can also inform what additional training or guidance you may need to give to your teaching staff.

Peer learning opportunities

There is a great opportunity to organise your team into pairs, triads or quads. The purpose of this is to support colleagues to be able to observe their peers. Teaching staff are often encouraged to observe peers in order to help them identify characteristics of effective teaching. Do your TAs get a similar opportunity to observe peers and gain an insight into how others carry out the role?

You need to consider the dynamics of each group when putting them together. Two fantastic TAs alongside someone who struggles to perform the role may present some issues. The gap in performance might be too vast so instead of being supportive, they may just continually see practices which they feel they are unable to deliver. Instead of being motivational, the grouping may well impact on the morale and motivation of individuals who do not feel they are as skilled as their peers. So, careful planning and consideration around the dynamics of each group is essential. We need to consider how colleagues will interact, communicate and support one another in a professional way.

If we want to get the most out of peer learning, we need to instil the sense of continuous improvement in how we undertake our roles. This is a journey we are going on. It is not about heading to a destination of 'outstanding' and then stopping, but a reflective process which leads to continuous improvement. It is an opportunity to ensure we are all able to learn from one another for the ultimate benefit of the learners we work with. This is not about judging but being curious about what we are seeing, posing questions, talking, exploring ideas and approaches and then identifying areas to further develop practice.

To mitigate against peer learning being used solely for making judgements on peers, you may need to model the process. What we don't want is our team being upset by comments made by their peers even if they are well-intended. If you model what the process looks like, then hopefully this will ensure clarity and consistency. You may well have to sit in on some observations and feedback in order to support the evolution of the process. The approach is very much steeped in coaching so some initial sessions getting staff to engage in coaching conversations will be helpful. Remember, for some, it might be a difficult experience because they are used to being told what to do or to giving advice. Again, this is about continuous improvement which is not solely focused on the views and guidance of one or two experts in a school setting.

Drip feed to reinforce the message

We know that one-off 'jazz hands' training sessions rarely lead to embedded change. However we decide to progress with our TA work, we need to consider how we will complement and reinforce our messages. We need to consider different approaches to communicating our intent that don't solely rely on a lectern or email.

One option you could consider is the potential of drip-feeding different advice and strategies to teaching staff and TAs over the academic year. If you develop a list of ways that TAs can support learners or be deployed around the classroom then these could be chunked and shared over time.

Consider these two different approaches to sharing information.

- **First approach:** you develop a list of twenty strategies, put them in one document and then share them with staff. They get some interest; staff read them, and some staff try out a few of the strategies from the list. However, most staff file the sheet away or leave it in a pigeonhole, they put the sheet to one side because there are too many strategies to consider.

- **Second approach:** you chunk your strategies from twenty individual points into ten pairs. Every fortnight you share another pair of strategies via the bulletin. There are only two strategies, so the suggestion is 'give them a try, see how you get on'. Every fortnight, you drip-feed another two strategies, so instead of reinforcing your message via one sheet on one occasion you are reminding colleagues over 20 weeks. You have also avoided cognitive overload by breaking the strategies down for your colleagues. You can revisit how the strategies are being implemented during staff meetings of training sessions.

Additional roles, non-financial motivation

The last consideration about TAs is in relation to what you can do to support individuals in being motivated in their role. Ideally, being a TA is seen as the start of a career and not just a job. TAs are generally not well-remunerated, sadly, and in a lot of situations their pay is beyond your control. What you can control are the conditions and the environment in which they work. This goes beyond bringing in cake and treats on a weekly basis.

Part of this will involve your strategic leadership and planning. It will involve you considering how you can adapt the role of the TA so there are opportunities for individuals to develop. Whilst you may not be able to influence pay, you can influence how well they are trained, developed and supported to evolve and further develop their skills, knowledge and expertise.

We could look at the additional provision we need in our setting (see Chapter 4) and then develop roles and responsibilities around those areas where we feel less supported or less skilled in. For example, if we know we struggle to access support from speech and language we might develop a position where someone is trained to be our in-house specialist. We get expertise and insight into learners' difficulties more promptly and we (hopefully) get a TA who feels valued and committed to their role who is more likely to stay with us.

Reflection time

What do you believe is the ideal role of the TA?

_____
_____
_____
_____
_____
_____
_____

Jot down a few ideas to support your first draft of a mission statement – you can share this with your team and refine later on.

_____
_____
_____
_____
_____
_____
_____

What is the gap between your ideal TA role and current practice?

_____
_____
_____
_____
_____
_____
_____

Outline the actions you need to take in order to raise awareness of what effective TA deployment involves.

_____

_____

_____

_____

_____

_____

_____

List your initial observations around the current deployment of TAs – what is working well and what are areas to develop?

_____

_____

_____

_____

_____

_____

Which members of staff can be your champions to highlight and celebrate effective TA and teacher practice?

_____

_____

_____

_____

_____

_____

What steps do you need to take in order to make sure peer learning groups are effective?

_____

_____

_____

_____

_____

_____

_____

What different forms of communication will you use to reinforce and remind staff about the role of TAs?

_____

_____

_____

_____

_____

_____

_____

Consider the additional responsibilities that could be offered to TAs to help support morale and motivation.

_____

_____

_____

_____

_____

_____

_____

10 Leading teaching and learning

Leading teaching and learning

We covered high-quality teaching in an earlier chapter. High-quality teaching we established was essential because it is the first line of intervention. If learners have access to great teachers who have high expectations for every learner and who consistently deliver high-quality teaching, then that is going to have the biggest impact on them, their progress and outcomes. There is also likely to be less need for additional interventions. Defining high-quality teaching and sharing it with staff across your setting is one thing; supporting reflection and the continuous improvement of teaching practices is another thing.

High-quality teaching needs to be a continual focus for SENCos and all leaders across the school. It is the essential strong foundation you refer to throughout the working week and across the academic year. Before you engage in escalating issues, come back to the teaching and learning experience to gain that valuable contextual insight. Therefore, leading teaching and learning is an imperative focus and an ongoing priority.

Perfect partnership?

When we went through developing high-quality teaching, we explored the relationship between the teaching and learning lead and you as the SENCo (unless you are one and the same; this should still be relevant though). Part of the challenge is not duplicating each other's efforts but working in a way that ensures your actions complement one another.

A good starting point will be sharing key priorities and draft action plans. In busy environments we know that it is sometimes easier to get your head down, do the work and then it gets done. The problem is that it gets done in isolation and might not fit in with the other pieces of the jigsaw puzzle you are continually trying to solve.

Sharing and comparing action plans can then help ensure that we achieve key priorities but perhaps with less effort, less time and fewer resources. Instead of working hard we work effectively and really consider how each action, each piece of work we undertake fits into the bigger picture. We have the opportunity to allocate key roles and responsibilities and pool resources in order to achieve our aims. We also have the added bonus of having a colleague to meet, share observations and progress with, and explore the next logical steps to take, given where you both agree you have got to.

It is important to mention again: Trust is important but agreement is not. Just because you don't agree doesn't make you adversaries, it makes you opponents. Adversaries are individuals with whom you do not trust and do not agree with. Fundamentally you stand for different things and it is unlikely that you will ever be on the same page with your thinking and actions. You are unlikely to benefit from engaging with adversaries because you don't trust their motives and you disagree with their philosophy around education. Great opponents help us improve what we are doing: we up our game in the face of constructive challenge. We trust our opponents and believe that their motives and intentions come from a positive place. The fact they disagree with your approaches is not a bad thing; your challenge is to reflect on how you can revise and refine your plans, so they are clearer. If you simply nod and agree without challenge, you risk undertaking actions that are simply wrong or ill thought out. That challenge is essential feedback to help us have clear and well-informed plans before we share them more widely with staff.

Common knowledge does not mean common practice

This is a key consideration when thinking about how you lead on teaching and learning. You need to be able to differentiate between what staff say they do and what they actually do in the classroom. If you have explored and defined what high-quality teaching is for your setting, you then need to venture out to see the reality over time.

Our curiosity about what we are seeing in lessons can help us gather information which can help influence our planning and future actions. Getting out into lessons gives us a fact-based approach to our work and not an anecdotal one. If we ever get questioned about the quality of teaching for learners with SEND and we respond with 'I think' we may be setting ourselves up for a grilling.

Do we think or do we know? Knowing helps us to be informed and aware, supporting our leadership decision-making. Anecdotal evidence can well lead to us being misinformed and then misdirected with our leadership.

Joint understanding

If you undertake some joint learning walks with your teaching and learning lead, then you can ensure that you are on the same page. When you walk through different classrooms, are you both of a similar view as to what you are seeing? No problem if you aren't: this could be a developmental opportunity for each party. The challenge is gradually aligning your views so that when you communicate with others, you do so with clarity and consistency in the message you share. This then avoids confusion amongst your staff, because you speak one language when it comes to high-quality teaching.

Where I undertake joint learning walks, I always find it interesting to get insight from others. Their views often give me food for thought and provide additional insight which I had not observed or considered. I think they are a great learning opportunity and one that I feel helps you to make better use of your peripheral vision to see and consider things you might otherwise have not thought about.

Andragogy not pedagogy

We are working with adults, each adult is bringing with them some sort of an opinion, knowledge and some degree of experience. The onus is really on them to take responsibility for their own learning and professional development. In this respect we need to reflect upon our role in structuring and supporting professional development for our colleagues.

This is very much a reflection from sitting through several whole school INSETs as a teacher and having to endure slide after slide which in no way provoked any reflection or thinking around a specific topic. How can we get individuals to take responsibility for their own learning if we don't design our training in that way?

Our role moves from one of teacher to facilitator. We know colleagues are coming with some prior knowledge. Our challenge is to gauge the different levels of experience, share some theory and then create opportunities for reflection, so that individuals can gauge the next steps for their own development. The responsibility is down to the individual, we just need to create the right conditions for them to want to engage. This includes the training sessions we deliver to colleagues. Staff can't be passive recipients, they need to be actively engaged, sharing ideas, discussing, collaborating, agreeing or disagreeing, but in all respects moving forward with their understanding.

It might be worthwhile looking at adult learning models such as Boyatzis' Intentional Change Theory or Glaser's Designing and Facilitating Adult Learning (in addition to the EEF implementation guide) to help you reflect on what good planning of professional development and learning can involve. CUREE are also an invaluable source of research into high quality, effective professional development and learning in education. The adult learning models and research from CUREE can support in ensuring that any approach is cyclical with you identifying dates to revisit themes as well as opportunities to introduce additional theory which will deepen understanding. This cycle also needs to include opportunities to share experiences of what it was like to actually put into practice the theory. This can help support peer learning but also highlight that mistakes may have been made but that they provided opportunities for reflection and further growth.

What makes great professional learning and development

This builds on the above paragraphs. We know from research that one-off events are unlikely to make a real difference to classroom practices. The guidance from the Department for Education laid out in the 'Standard for teachers' professional development' July 2016 sets the standard in the following headings (in bold), followed by my commentary.

1. Professional development should have a focus on improving and evaluating pupil outcomes.

This brings us back to context: if you are going to improve outcomes for your learners, you need to know what your starting point is. What are the barriers experienced by the learners in your own context? What can you do to upskill staff so they are better able to engage and support learners with acquiring knowledge and learning new skills?

2. Professional development should be underpinned by robust evidence and expertise.

Evidence and expertise are important, and it is essential they work in tandem. Evidence is great but if it is not applied in the right way then it is not going to have the desired impact. The expertise is essentially the synthesis aspect of understanding the research and being able to make sense of it so it can be applied expertly in a learning environment. I like to think of this process as being 'evidence-informed but practice-refined'. The expert input can help us understand how to make approaches work better when we adopt them.

3. Professional development should include collaboration and expert challenge.

Collaboration helps us feel that we are not in this alone and that we have colleagues to share and discuss ideas with as part of our learning journey. Organising staff into quads or triads helps formalise this so that conversations and the sharing of learning is planned rather than accidental. These staff groupings can also add an element of challenge to the process. Colleagues can agree development points with regards to specific pedagogical practices. These can then be revisited with learning reflections shared and then the opportunity to discuss other approaches which may also help individuals to further develop their practices. You could even facilitate peer observations or lesson study so that you observe one another teaching and then share key observations which again help refine the use of strategies used in the learning environment.

4. Professional development programmes should be sustained over time.

We have already mentioned that professional learning needs to be sustained over time. You need to discern between quality versus quantity. The less is more approach is a key consideration here. This is not about covering lots of different areas of SEND and expecting staff to retain it all. This is about identifying your key priorities and then ensuring they are the focus for the year. Threading in opportunities to revisit and share learning will help ensure staff don't revert back to old habits. If you have a sustained focus, colleagues will know this is not a fad or temporary focus but something that supports continued professional development and learning. You can make sure that the challenge is in every member of staff having to share their learning in one forum or another. This can also be factored into departmental meetings where your middle leaders explore how your current focus is being applied across all your classrooms.

5. Professional development must be prioritised by school leadership.

Prioritising professional development and learning as a school leadership team is essential if you want to ensure all your staff embrace research and new practices. It is not only a case of prioritising professional development but also being seen to be actively engaged in it themselves. If you are organising professional learning for staff, then part of your preparation has to include inviting all members of the school leadership team. This helps set a precedent across the school that attendance is non-negotiable. It communicates that you are all part of a learning community who all need to continue to develop and learn over time so that you can give your learners the best possible experiences in school.

You need to endorse and embody the principle of lifelong learning and that you can all learn even if it does involve revisiting topics you have previously covered.

Supporting autonomy

Whilst there is a central approach adopted in many schools in which professional learning is directive, you may need to consider alternative approaches which support staff autonomy. There are schools which have teaching and learning research groups which focus in on particular themes identified in school development plans. Groups are organised by senior staff, focus areas are shared and time is then allocated for professional learning. Straightforward, but let's think of other ways you can go about doing this which might motivate staff more.

Consider splitting this down into:

Task

Is it possible for staff to engage with a topic that is linked with school development priorities? Considering individual motivation, if someone is interested in a topic, they are more likely to want to engage with it. You may need to highlight the importance of each topic or theme so that individuals can also identify the longer-term benefits of engaging with it.

Team

Can you let staff organise who they would like to work with? I know you may have put some staff in quads or triads for teaching and learning but for the purposes of research groups you could offer the opportunity for staff to work with colleagues who they feel will support and challenge them in equal measures.

Technique

'Learn from your mistakes' is something we often say to learners, encouraging them to take risks but also reflecting on what went wrong and what could be done differently in the future. You need to apply this same principle to your research groups. Give them the space to engage in experiential learning so they learn as they go along. Tempting as it is to tinker and influence approaches used by groups, you need to let them learn from their own approaches and possible mistakes. If you tinker or get too involved then you risk limiting their progress and eventual outcomes to their own experiences, knowledge and understanding of issues. You could be missing out on new approaches if you limit groups to using your thinking or that of other leaders.

Time

Our research groups used to take place on a Monday after school, which for me was the worst day of the week and the time when I had the least amount of energy. Rather than dictate when groups should meet, could you give a minimum expectation of the amount of time they need to focus on their task? Teams and individuals within them can then decide when they are most productive and can then focus their efforts during those times. No point making people work when they are in a cognitive trough because that is likely to be frustrating and not very productive.

If you get the four Ts right then you aren't just ensuring you have your teams focusing on key areas for development in a productive manner, you are also improving the conditions in which your staff are working. Your trust is communicating that as professionals you know best, you know how to approach your work, when to approach it and with whom to approach it. Yes, you will check in and seek updates but ultimately this is down to you, the professionals in our school. This can then have a significantly positive impact on morale and motivation as well as outcomes for your learners.

In addition to some of the positives mentioned above, you are also creating champions of teaching and learning. Each group will have key individuals in them who will be developing their confidence and ability to speak on key areas of pedagogy and great classroom practice. These individuals then become your champions to share the message about great teaching and learning. You are effectively distributing leadership so that this doesn't become an area that a few people lead on but an area where several leaders are focusing their efforts and attention on a daily basis. Think about the culture being developed where individuals invest in their own development and support the learning and development of their peers in a reciprocal manner.

Using data to target support

In addition to working with the teaching and learning lead you also need to consider the role your data lead can play in targeting where additional support may be necessary. Your data should be able to give you an insight into the classes where your learners with SEND do well and where they do less well. This is not about judging those teachers on data alone, but it is a starting point which can help you to be curious about the possible reasons why learners with SEND do less well.

Once you have the data you can work with your colleagues to ensure you visit specific classrooms during your learning walks. You can then (over time) start developing an understanding of what you are all seeing and how this might fit into an overall hypothesis. This can also be backed up through conversations with staff to explore their views on how well learners are doing and if there are any particular learners who may need additional support and/or guidance, or the same for parts of their teaching.

This approach can help ensure that you can be more targeted and nuanced in your approach to leading teaching and learning. While you may give a standard talk at staff training sessions, you need to ensure you know how it lands and has been received and understood at an individual level.

Working with our middle leaders

Teaching and learning is the responsibility of every member of staff, not just senior leaders. You need to think about how you can fully utilise the skills, knowledge and experience of your middle leaders so they reinforce key messages around teaching and learning. Every interaction is an opportunity to discuss teaching and learning. If you have middle leaders talking consistently about teaching and learning, then you are more likely to be able to embed your whole school approach.

Subject or phase meetings also provide an ideal opportunity to discuss pedagogy and practice across your teams. If an issue is raised – perhaps around behaviour, rather than get drawn into the behaviour and possible consequences, you can be curious and explore the antecedents. This does not mean you excuse any poor behaviour; it is more the case that middle leaders are gathering additional context. What was happening beforehand? What was the teacher doing? What was the learner doing? Part of this is also about slowing down and exploring key triggers or recurring patterns of behaviour. If others in your department are having similar experiences, then consider what you need to try in order to adapt your approach.

If you have middle leaders adopting a position of curiosity, then you can explore and understand what additional training or support our staff may need in terms of classroom practice. This is not about judging; if colleagues feel they are being judged then they are less likely to share what has gone on. You need open and honest dialogue so that middle leaders have a clear understanding of strengths and areas for improvement across their team. It might be that with this clarity they use meeting times as an opportunity for professional learning which will better target the needs of their team.

Knowledge of change management

It is worth researching change management to have an accurate understanding of the different ways colleagues might well react to change. The EEF have their implementation guidance which outlines a process which can help introduce and embed change. It is also worth looking into Kotter's 8 stage change model which will help you reflect on the planning and actions you will need to undertake if change is going to be sustained.

What is worth considering is the approach you will take with the whole staff and then the approach you may need to take with individuals. Different members of staff are going to react and respond in different ways; therefore, the approach you will need is going to be different. You can see the change process as a cycle of peak, trough, peak. What will help colleagues reach the other peak is the individual conversations you have, which will encourage them and remind them of the overall vision you are all working towards. Again, this is a leadership action you will need to undertake to support colleagues going through the overall process. In some respects, this is you personalising your approach to meet the individual needs of your teaching staff.

The next chapter gives some practical strategies that will help you plan out any changes to help ensure they become embedded across your setting.

Reflection time

What are your key priorities for leading teaching and learning in your school?

_____
_____
_____
_____
_____
_____
_____

How do your priorities link in with those of the senior team / whole school?

_____
_____
_____
_____
_____
_____
_____

From your understanding of existing classroom practice, what is going to be the essential first step you take with staff training?

_____
_____
_____
_____
_____
_____
_____

What steps can you take to empower your staff to take more responsibility for their own professional development and learning?

_____
_____
_____
_____
_____
_____
_____

What are your own development needs for leading teaching and learning? How can you address these over the academic year?

_____
_____
_____
_____
_____
_____
_____

How might you differentiate or personalise your leadership of teaching and learning for individual members of staff?

_____
_____
_____
_____
_____
_____
_____

How will you address situations where individuals are not engaging with professional development? Who will you need to work with to address this?

_____

_____

_____

_____

_____

_____

_____

11 Making change stick

Change is complex

Change is complex; we aren't just changing or introducing a new idea or way of working. What we are doing is looking to influence behaviours and practices and get individuals to embrace different approaches. These behaviours and practices didn't evolve overnight, so nor will they change overnight. We need to therefore consider the approaches we plan to take in order to bring about sustained change in our setting.

One-off events are unlikely to affect long term change. They might appear to be well received but after the applause fades people are likely to go back to doing what they were doing beforehand. The challenge therefore is to consider a range of complementary activities that will help sustain change over the academic year and beyond. If we don't back up our initial 'launch' then colleagues are likely to revert back to old habits, especially when no one is watching.

We are dealing with complexity here which means there is a degree of uncertainty, so getting to X is not necessarily going to get you to Y. In some respects what we are doing is engaging in an experiment in which, although we have an ideal outcome in mind, there are lots of variables at play which are going to impact on us achieving some of our small-step outcomes. We are going to have to be agile and intelligent with our thinking and actions so that we can change strategies and approaches in light of small-step progress and ongoing feedback from various stakeholders.

Be mindful of the ego

Before you progress, you need to address the issue of ego and how this might impact on any progress you make with your changes. The experiment you are asking your colleagues to engage with presents a risk. New ways of working are different; they present a risk in that some individuals will see themselves as effective, competent practitioners. Doing things differently may mean that they get different outcomes, especially in the short term. These different outcomes (in the short term) may be seen as undesirable, such as deteriorating behaviour or a change in classroom dynamics. This is going to be tough to take, especially if individuals feel they are getting decent results already.

We often speak to learners about taking risks and that if we fail, we can learn from our mistakes. But how often do we see colleagues willing to take a risk? Equally, what will be the perceived ramifications or consequences if they do take a risk and they fail? Again, the anxiety beforehand is often much worse than the reality but how often have you seen it inhibit individuals in taking more risks in the classroom?

On a professional level what will happen to members of staff who take risks, but things don't work out so well. Will you be supporting them with conversations of encouragement and exploring how to adapt approaches so that success is more likely in the future? If they know they will be supported, then that might help them take risks. If, however, they feel it is going to turn into a capability issue, then they might be more inclined to stick with what they know and feel they do best even if it is not great.

On a teaching and learning level the risks of failing will impact on progress and engagement. You need to somehow reassure individuals and groups that by changing and refining practices progress and engagement will be more likely to improve in the longer-term. The impact of not being willing to take a risk is that you maintain the current status quo which is perhaps not serving every learner as best as it can do.

In some respects, being good is going to create some inertia when you are looking to evolve, adapt or change practices or approaches in your setting. People are not going to necessarily appreciate the possible long-term benefits they will experience when the short-term pain seems to come, quite possibly at a high cost. So, in some respects your enemy is 'good' because good is OK, good is acceptable. We have all been led to believe and accept that good is fine when really, we should have our sights set much higher. We should all want great things for our staff, our learners and wider school community.

Support from leadership

To mitigate against the potential inertia, we need support from other leaders across our setting, from senior and middle leaders to classroom and support staff leaders. In some respects, we need our leaders to share their vulnerabilities and concerns about moving forward with new practices. This can humanise and legitimise anxiety so that all staff can feel reassured (to a degree) that what they are feeling is not unique to them. Equally, this can help ensure that as we progress it is in the spirit of 'We, Us, Together!'.

The involvement of leadership can also help ensure that there is a consistent message of support as you progress. You can agree how you will all respond to staff concerns and how you can support and encourage all staff to continue to embrace new approaches or classroom practices. This might even extend to praising risk-takers regardless of outcome. The idea will be that any risks are reflected on and discussed to help individuals identify the next steps they need to take as part of their ongoing development.

Leadership and your vision

It might be helpful for you to consider how you will use your leadership to influence behaviours and practices. Whether you are on the senior leadership team or not, you have a leadership role to perform. It might be worth thinking about how you are going to show up in different situations and how you might respond to different staff reactions. How will you respond in a rational, measured response, even if it feels like a colleague is not being rational or reasonable themselves?

This takes us back to differentiating our leadership style given the individual we are interacting with. We need to be realistic in that not everyone is going to be necessarily that happy about having to change. You have probably heard countless conversations of how everything in education goes round in cycles. Some individuals might approach change with a jaded and somewhat unenthusiastic attitude because they feel they have gone through it all before. This takes us back to our first chapter and the importance of having a clear vision. Your leadership and your responses need to circle back to the vision. What you are doing is going to help the whole school community on your journey to improve outcomes for your most vulnerable learners. This is not a personal attack on individuals, this is about wanting to continually improve everyone's practices because they are going to make a huge difference to all your learners.

Plan it like a project not a task

Everyone has their own approach to planning, but I would suggest moving beyond a document that rarely sees the light of day. We need to scale this differently because of the complex nature of change. You have an opportunity to make use of project management techniques which can help you to scope out a range of activities and actions that you and your colleagues will undertake across an academic year. This can also help you to see see how different activities and actions complement each other in order to support the change process.

Another benefit of adopting a project management approach is that it can help avoid silo working. If you reflect on how action plans and development plans are often implemented, what you often see is leaders at various levels creating action plans with targets to work towards. What this doesn't do is show an overall picture of how everything knits together for a coherent plan for change. In some respects, this silo working contributes to the duplication of time, effort and resources as each individual seeks to achieve what they need for their particular area of responsibility. A project management approach can give you more of a holistic picture of what is going on and identify the contributions of staff beyond their own immediate teams.

Project logic

Project logic provides a framework that will help us scope out what you need to do to help achieve your outcomes. It gives you key things to consider before you even undertake your planning or project mapping. These key considerations are:

Objective

What do you want to achieve? This needs to be measurable so you can objectively gauge the progress made as a result of the activities that have been undertaken. This objective should be linked in some way with your vision so you can clearly articulate the importance of working towards achieving this objective.

Actions

Outline the different actions you need to take in order to give yourself and your colleagues a chance of making progress with your objective. Clearly detail the work needed to be undertaken across the academic year. Include preparatory work you will need to do before you even step in front of staff to share plans and actions. You can also add in initials here to indicate who is responsible for specific tasks or actions.

Deliverables

This is a 'so what?' focus. If you undertake all this work, then what do you get as a result? For instance, if you focus on improving high-quality teaching you might get better rates of progress for learners (which you could break down into sub-groups for clear tracking). You might also get a central bank of strategies that all staff use to support their classroom teaching. Essentially, these deliverables are a direct result of your work.

Benefits

Sometimes, when you undertake work, you get a by-product; something positive that you might not have intended to achieve. Some benefits of improving high-quality teaching might be less disruption in lessons or improved attendance as learners feel more able to access learning in the classroom. You might even have a reduction in the number of interventions running as more needs are being met in the classroom. All these are benefits but not necessarily what you were originally setting out to achieve.

Key Performance Indicators

Key Performance Indicators (KPIs) are going to be your data: clear, objective statistics that will help you measure progress by fact, not anecdote. You could also include some qualitative data (staff or student voice) here alongside your quantitative to give a broader understanding of the progress being made.

Critical Success Factors

Critical Success Factors (CSFs) are the things that are essential to have in place in order for you to succeed. Sometimes you might be hindered with your plans by not having the right budget, people, resources or time. This is an opportunity to be really clear with leaders. If your objective is something you all really want to achieve, then you must have these critical success factors in place. After all, how many plans fail because you are cutting corners, making do with outdated equipment or materials or having your time with staff cut short because something has come up?

You can create a table to help plan out your ideas, working with colleagues to discuss the different activities that could take place over the academic year.

This is essentially your preparation that will be invaluable when it comes to planning out your project.

Objective	Actions	Deliverable	Benefits	KPIs	CSFs

Make it dynamic, plan with your colleagues

This is where the project logic feeds into your project management. You have the opportunity to dispense with laptops and use huge sheets of paper. Cover a whole wall with paper and then view it as your academic year. What can you do over an academic year that will help ensure you achieve your objectives as well as embed them? This is an opportunity to plan out your journey, take a step back, discuss with colleagues and then add in other activities that will help you make progress.

Flexibility can be built into this process by using sticky notes to indicate dates you need activities started or finished by. Labels for staff can also be added to the planning to indicate who is responsible for tasks. As this is a dynamic planning process, you can take a step back, see your plan developing and then talk through how it is progressing and whether given your discussions you need to shift dates or staff around. This gives you all a realistic overview of what you actually need to do over an academic year.

You have collaborated, discussed and disagreed but (hopefully) have reached a point where you have consensus around what you all feel is the best way to proceed. What you haven't done is work tirelessly on your own to type up a plan that colleagues might not commit to, even if you have included their names on it.

Don't let it get dusty

The benefit of having your plan on a huge piece of paper is that you can bring it out and revisit how you are doing at different points across the academic year. You can discuss progress, take stock of where you or colleagues are up to and if necessary, change activities, timings or the staff involved. This is the opposite of being dogmatic, where people progress with their original plans regardless of progress, timescales or impact.

You get the opportunity to continue to collaborate, to share responsibility, to benefit from insight from colleagues so that your plans have a greater chance of succeeding. The act of revisiting and adjusting your plans helps to ensure they remain agile, flexing your approach in light of where you are up to rather than ploughing ahead and ignoring what all the data and feedback is telling you. You also have the benefit of hindsight which you didn't have when you originally devised your plan. Ask yourself: Knowing what you know now, what do you and your colleagues need to do differently?

Get the paper out and use it for reflection and discussion, but more importantly, use it to focus your effort and energy. Do work that is going to make a difference and lead to change not just work that is going to keep you busy but achieves little impact.

Enable control and ownership

Whilst you may have identified actions and activities that need to be undertaken to achieve your objective try to consider how you can empower colleagues to take control and own the activities. Part of this might be built on trust but have a think about what you can do to help people own and be proud of the work they are undertaking.

This brings us back to differentiating your leadership given the context and the individuals you are working with. If you are clear about what needs to be done, then you can perhaps take a step back and allow colleagues the space to get on with it. If you have competent colleagues, then looking over their shoulder every minute is perhaps going to be counter-productive and casts you as an overbearing individual. Yes, you may need to do this with some colleagues but don't have it as a blanket default approach.

Think about the leadership style you are going to use so that you empower colleagues and get the best out of them. Remember, leadership is about the influence you have on others, it is not about you doing all the work to the detriment of your own responsibilities and health.

Move beyond emails

In order to sustain momentum, you also need to consider how you communicate progress and developments with your stakeholders (staff, learners, governors, parents). Communication helps you to avoid your work becoming another new initiative that is forgotten about mid-year. Take some time to think about the different forms of communication you can use to keep everyone abreast of developments. Think about how you can keep the excitement, enthusiasm and interest ticking over across the year.

It may be that you think about the different stakeholders and consider the best way to target them. In a busy world, emails often seem an expedient tool to share information but how many people really read them?

You can consider the different mediums you might use, and which audience would most benefit from that format. For instance, governors might like to read reports about the progress you are making. You can update staff through morning briefings. Parents could be updated and kept abreast of developments via the school's newsletters. Parent consultation evenings might be an opportunity to advertise key developments or run a short video on loop to show what is happening across the school. You just need to be clear as to what different stakeholders are likely to engage with so that your time and effort in communicating is outweighed by the effect they have on others.

Find your champions for follow-up training

Whilst we have said that one-off training is unlikely to bring about sustained change, it doesn't have to be down to you to deliver follow-up training. Consider which members of staff are onboard or have been adopting the approaches you have suggested. These individuals are effectively your champions who can extol the benefits they have experienced by engaging with new approaches or by trying out different strategies.

Think about this from a neutral perspective, if you stand up in front of staff for a follow-up session and share the great progress you have seen, how is that going to be perceived? If you are objective, this means the person who introduced the new ways of working (possibly with a vested interest) is standing up to tell everyone what a success the new ways have been. You risk being seen as disingenuous because colleagues may assume you want your work to look good.

Instead, consider having a member of staff sharing their experience to date. They can share their experiences, initial anxieties, successes and areas that they want to finesse in the future. This shares out responsibility and takes some of the pressure away from you in feeling you always have to deliver training. It means you have also developed another voice who is advocating for inclusion and the changes you have introduced, sharing how they can actually make a positive difference. If you can do this for subsequent sessions then you can see how you can go from the SENCo manager to the SENCo leader, influencing behaviours across the whole school.

Reflection time

What might be some of the barriers experienced by colleagues to engaging with your proposals? What can you do to mitigate these barriers?

_____
_____
_____
_____
_____
_____
_____

How do your proposals link back to your SEND vision and why are they necessary?

_____
_____
_____
_____
_____
_____
_____

Which members of staff are you going to involve in creating your project plan? (Consider trust and agreement to ensure you receive a healthy level of challenge.)

_____
_____
_____
_____
_____
_____
_____

When are you going to revisit your project plan? Which colleagues will you revisit it with? (Stick these dates and names in your calendar to avoid slippage.)

_____
_____
_____
_____
_____
_____
_____

Outline the different ways you are going to communicate the ongoing progress of your project to different stakeholders.

_____
_____
_____
_____
_____
_____
_____

What criteria will you use to select your champions? (Can anyone else help you to identify them?)

_____
_____
_____
_____
_____
_____
_____

12 The coaching SENCo

It's OK to give advice

Just like there are several leadership styles, there are a range of ways you can support your colleagues. You use different leadership styles depending on the context and individual. The consideration is whether the particular leadership styles you choose are effective. According to Goleman, there are six different leadership styles: coercive/directive, authoritative, pacesetting, affiliative, democratic and coaching. However, we often err towards ones we feel most comfortable with. Similarly, there are different ways in which you can support staff, but do you go to a particular default response?

There are times when, given the situation (perhaps where time is at a premium), you may need to dispense advice and get the issue resolved. It may also be the case that the individual you are working with does not have the experience to come up with an answer they have confidence in. In this situation, mentoring might be a more appropriate approach where you talk through options then share your experience.

The reflection for you as a leader is: Over a given week when people come to you with a problem, dilemma or issue, how do you respond? Do you use a variety of approaches, or do you have a go-to response because it is convenient and provides an expedient end to the matter? For a simple reflection activity think about your interactions with staff. When they come to you with an issue on how many occasions do you give the answer and on how many occasions do they come up with the answer? Are you inadvertently creating a dependency culture which will result in you being continually busy and in demand?

Let others go first

One final consideration: at which point do you share your advice, guidance or solutions with others? If you have decided that this is going to be an advice-giving interaction (which is fine) then you may want to initially hold back on giving your advice. It might be more helpful and provide an opportunity to build confidence if you get your colleague to share their solutions first.

You can say 'Sounds like this is troubling you, what ideas do you have for overcoming it?'. In this approach you make the focus on the individual explaining the issue and then taking ownership for possible solutions. The reason you want them to speak first is so you can get an idea of the actual problem as they perhaps explain a little bit more about it than they initially disclosed. You also get an idea about their thinking process and how they might tackle issues. Finally, the other reason you don't want to share your ideas first is because of the 'top trump' effect. You are the one with the experience, knowledge and expertise, so when you share your ideas first, then they may feel that there is little point in carrying on the conversation because you have shared what you have thought about the matter. I.e., some colleagues might see that as a full stop and end to the conversation because what else can they add to rival your wisdom?

Busy, busy, busy

I run SENCo leadership training programmes and one of my sessions focuses on time management. When I ask delegates to write down what they did the previous week, it is sometimes easier to get them to list what they didn't do. Schools like many other places of employment are busy but being a SENCo in a school feels like a different level of busy-ness.

When we go through the time management quadrant so many activities and tasks get squeezed in to the majority of the boxes. The four sections are:

1. Urgent and important
2. Not urgent but important
3. Urgent but not important
4. Not urgent and not important

It might be worth undertaking this exercise yourself to help you reflect on where your time is being spent or taken up over the course of a working week. How much time do you get to focus on the tasks you need to do? This might also include a reflection on how you divide your time between operational aspects of the role and focusing on strategic opportunities and developments that will bring about longer-term improvements.

Back to the time management. Part of the reflections are around whether other people's approaches to time management impact on your working practices. For instance, if someone operates on a last-minute basis then any requests from them are likely to fall into 'urgent and important', i.e. more time pressure and extra work for you. In this situation a conversation about their practices and how they might be incompatible with your practices might be helpful. It could be uncomfortable, but it is going to be helpful. It might be the case the other person is oblivious to the impact their own working practices are having on others so at least you have brought it out into the open.

Equally, how many people come to you with something they feel is urgent and important but when you dig a little deeper it is not actually that important? This might be someone seeking your support because Child X has kicked off again and they feel that only you, the 'Super SENCo', can resolve the situation. It's great to feel needed and your nurturing nature likes to be helpful but are you overlooking a possible training need? Is your approach the equivalent of putting a plaster over what could be a substantial wound?

The final reflection around working in a busy environment is whether your interactions with others perpetuate how busy you are. Could it be that you are taking short-term approaches which save time, at that point in time? Are you potentially putting off adopting or introducing leadership practices because whilst you know there will be long-term benefits, these seem to be far outweighed by the short-term (maybe even medium-term) pain of changing your own behaviour?

Leadership PPA

Before we progress on from time management you may want to consider when you do your best thinking. What time of the day or day of the week is it? This is a consideration for you because this is going to be the difference between you working operationally or creating space to work strategically. This is really about giving yourself permission to take time across the week to focus on strategic leadership.

Consider what would happen if you took away PPA time from teaching staff, think about the impact on staff, teaching and learning and outcomes for learners. Also, things would stop progressing, there would be practices adopted that may no longer meet the needs of learners. Now use that thinking and apply it to your leadership or even the practices used to support SEND across your setting.

You do need to give yourself permission to take time to think strategically. Yes, there will be individuals that will always need you across the week which might create a sense of guilt but you need to create time and space so you can think about what will be different and better in the future. Allow yourself some dedicated time in a week where you are going to focus on strategy and considering how you and your colleagues can progress to your vision. This is an investment in the future and an opportunity to break the status quo, don't feel guilty, you need this headspace time to evolve and further develop SEND and inclusion practices across your setting.

Don't get hung up on the term 'coaching'

Let's start off by dispelling any concerns you may have around coaching. There is a lot out there on coaching, some of it really helpful and easy to access, some of it complicated and quite complex. Ignore the latter and focus on the former. Coaching is essentially an interaction in which you are using questions and curiosity to better understand someone's situation or context. You have to listen, be in the moment and use questions to dig deeper. In some respects, you are a detective, using questions to get to the truth and listening to responses to work out what your next line of enquiry will be.

You may have been involved in mentoring students or colleagues, which was a skill you had to develop and refine over time. Coaching is going to be the same: it is a skill that you need to focus attention on, engage in deliberate practice of, probably make mistakes but you will get better over time. We will explore why it is going to be an essential skill to have when it comes to developing sustainable work practices.

Ask a few more questions before progressing

Part of the challenge is changing your habit of how you respond when people present you with an issue. Quite possibly your ingrained behaviour is to immediately come up with an answer or solution. After all, you are a teacher, your job is to help and to educate. It is also highly likely you are a nurturing individual who wants to look after or look out for colleagues. You want to do what you can to make their lives easier because teaching is after all a challenging vocation.

When you are conditioned to respond with answers, you risk missing out key information that might help you to better understand the root cause of an issue. What you might have to do is pose a few more questions to find out the bigger picture. Additional context can provide you with a better insight into what the underlying issues might be for the individual seeking your advice, support or help. It might even be helpful to establish what they want to get from the conversation from the outset. You can then decide the most appropriate course of action to take. Is this a tell them and get them on their way interaction or is this a situation where you need to listen, understand and then use questioning to deepen your understanding so that you can better support the individual. By support I mean taking the correct act of leadership which might not mean giving the individual the answer, but instead making them do the legwork to arrive at something they can own and progress with.

Tell me more

There is some interesting science out there around listening and speaking. We tend to think way faster than we are able to talk, so there is a high likelihood that what we initially say is not entirely what we mean, think or feel about a situation. If we adopt a 'tell me more' approach, we can elicit additional information which can help the other person to clarify their own thinking. This approach can help the individual make better sense of their predicament, which can support them in thinking about solutions to the actual 'whole' problem not just their first utterance. Your questioning can help the member of staff process what is actually going on in their head. We don't have to make sense of what they are saying, they do, because it is their issue.

What you are also doing with this 'tell me more' approach is creating time for the other person to think, talk and share their concerns, but also for us to listen. You can listen for what is being said and, perhaps more importantly, what is not being said. Your detective questioning skills can then help both of you to come to a situation where you understand most (if not all) of the problem. Once you have the 'real' problem then you can start thinking about how we can progress and come to some sort of resolution.

Your options

Once you have the 'real' problem out in the open, it is round about this time you are itching to 'help'. This is your moment to earn your money, show your greatness and prove how effective you are but this is the exact moment you need to restrain yourself and get the other person to take responsibility. In effect you have managed to get the reality of the situation by listening and just getting the other person to tell you more. The next step is exploring what might be a helpful way forward.

For this part of the conversation, you can simply ask:

- What options do you have?
- What does success look like here?
- What are you going to do about it?
- What does help for you involve?

Importantly only pose one question at a time so that the other person can focus on that question and come up with a well-thought-out response. This is an opportunity for you to move away from your 'Super SENCo' status and get the other person to think through what they can do to resolve or improve matters. This is your chance to give the other person responsibility for their own freedom when it comes to making decisions. They need to feel they can and (in many cases) should be coming up with the answers or right actions to take.

The temptation here is that you are so happy to hear one option that you take that as the only way forward. Remember, just like them sharing the problem, the first thing they say is not necessarily going to be the most useful or best way forward. You need more than one option so ask them to think of and share more with you.

- Could you do anything else?
- Any more ideas?
- What else?

Once you have a few ideas you can then explore what the possible merits and challenges involved with each option might be.

What does success look like?

You have options to consider, but in some respects this is just the beginning, you then need to take a 'so what?' approach. What does a successful outcome or resolution to this issue look like? Be really clear here on what the individual will be doing and what the other parties (perhaps learners in the classroom) will be doing. If these are ambiguous then they may well be open to interpretation, so get the other person to be really clear about what they mean and what they will do.

If you have several options, then what actions will the other person take in order to make them reality? Again, you need clarity here. You know what success looks like so you need to get your colleague to identify the necessary actions that will make this a reality. This is another opportunity for the other person to take responsibility for resolving the situation. It is important that they come up with ideas for the actions they are going to take because they are going to have to own them. They are the ones who are going to have to implement the actions and strategies, so they need to be clear as to what they will involve and what they will personally be doing.

If the criteria for success ends up being ambiguous, then measuring it is going to be subjective instead of objective. That's not very helpful when you are trying to establish what went well and what could be further improved upon. Do take time to focus in on and explore what 'better' looks like and involves so you have that objectivity when discussing it and also identifying it in practice.

Come back to the conversation

As busy as you are, don't let this be a one-off conversation. You have started a process here where a colleague has identified an issue, explored options and then agreed to undertake actions. You haven't resolved anything through that one conversation, nothing has changed. You need to agree a date when you can revisit this issue, talk through progress and explore other possible actions.

Hopefully, the second coaching interaction will shed even more light on the situation, so you get an even better understanding of what is really at play here. You also have an opportunity to see what actions the other person has actually taken to improve the situation. Remember, even though you are a caring colleague, this is not your problem, this is your colleague's problem, so ask yourself what they have done to improve things. Yes, you can be empathetic, but the only person who is going to bring about change is the person sharing their issue with you.

You can refer back to the initial conversation and discuss the proposed actions and what progress to date looks like along with any remaining challenges. There may well be some frustrations aired here because success might not be immediate, but you need to persist. If you are looking for an individual to change some of their practices, then it may take time to refine how they introduce them to their repertoire. You can identify next steps, what the other person will do, what success will look like and agree a date to revisit progress.

Remember, this whole approach is about you developing sustainable work practices, you need to hold your ground and commit to the process. There is little point in getting someone to think through options and ways forward if you always end up rescuing them before they have really tried to change their own practices or situation. Just like with learners, the struggle is an important part of the learning process. It is where our metacognition kicks in.

Don't fill the silence

One thing that can be uncomfortable when you pose a question is the ensuing silence. It might only be 10 seconds, but it feels like an eternity. You may be tempted to pose another question but don't. If you have posed a question asking someone to reflect on their practices or how they go about doing their job, then that is a tough question. It is going to take time to really think about what they do and how they might share this with you. Staying quiet allows them some thinking time, which might be something they haven't done much of before they have brought their problem to you.

Remember, the whole point of this coaching approach was to help avoid you being a bottleneck in the system because everyone comes to you for solutions. It may be that some questions don't get answered straight away, but that is fine as you can revisit them in a subsequent interaction. Staying quiet and not leaping in to rescue situations helps other process their thoughts and take responsibility for resolving matters. In a busy world, your silence is a gift to your colleague because you are allowing them time to actually think rather than react.

A question mark doesn't make it a coaching interaction

I've been fortunate enough to facilitate numerous leadership sessions where we have engaged in coaching. One of the biggest challenges I have seen is where experienced SENCos have struggled not to give advice. What starts off as a coaching session soon turns into mentoring. The 'cheating' begins when advice is posed as a question. For example, the question 'Have you thought about an ELSA?' does have a question mark, but for all intents and purposes it is sharing an answer to the issue.

Again, there is nothing wrong with mentoring and there is nothing wrong with sharing ideas. The reflection is whether you are perpetuating the demands being placed on your time by providing possible solutions to problems. In terms of self-advocacy, what are your colleagues doing to resolve a situation before they come to you? How are they using their own brains before they come and seek the wisdom of yours?

A ceiling on possibilities

One last reflection on coaching is that when you do it well, the other person comes up with a solution and a way forward. They might even come up with a solution you hadn't considered. If you don't engage in coaching and persist with giving advice and fixing situations, are you potentially limiting the practices that are adopted across your own setting? Does your own experience become the ceiling on possibilities, because when you give advice you are effectively controlling the practices across your setting? You are effectively limiting possibilities by linking solutions to your own experience, knowledge and wisdom.

Support high-quality teaching

Another opportunity you have is the potential to use coaching conversations as part of your daily interactions with colleagues. When you visit lessons, you can be curious, you can pose questions that will help colleagues reflect on their practice. Rather than have judgement-based approaches you can engage with colleagues by 'wondering' aloud. You can ask about the learning journey: what learners know and how this will support them understanding new topics. You can explore how learners might be engaging with tasks and how scaffolding might be supporting individuals to overcome any barriers they might have.

What might help in getting colleagues to engage with you is by entering their classrooms empty-handed. No clipboards, no tick sheets, just an open mind, wondering about what is happening in the classroom and how this links in with the high-quality teaching you have articulated across your setting. You have a couple of options open to you, you can engage in a conversation with the member of staff in the lesson, but this might interrupt the flow of the lesson. The other option is that you can touch base with the individual later in the day and have a brief conversation about what was going on. Any lesson visit is a snapshot over time: your role here is to remain open and curious and pose questions that will support professional reflection and may influence practices in the future.

One last point here is the importance of conversation. I have seen several settings that issue a tick sheet after a lesson has been visited to indicate what the observer saw. This sometimes links to the EEF's 5 a day (explicit instruction, cognitive and meta-cognitive strategies, scaffolding, flexible grouping and using technology). Again, nothing wrong with this but it is a quantitative measure whereas a conversation offers a qualitative measure and more clarity. The conversation helps support reflection and discussion around other pedagogical approaches that might be useful in the future. A tick sheet isn't going to achieve that same level of reflection or consideration for the future just because one box never gets ticked.

Consider the self-scaffolding model

In chapter 9, we looked at the self-scaffolding model that TAs can use with learners. The model has several layers:

- self-scaffolding
- prompting
- clueing
- modelling
- correcting.

Let's take a step back and consider how this model works when as a SENCo you interact with colleagues. Take some time to reflect for a minute on how interactions normally play out when a colleague approaches you with an issue. As a former SENCo I know there are individuals who quite often seek advice or guidance in relation to specific classroom issues or individual learners. Play these interactions over in your mind and consider what your initial reactions are when someone brings an issue to you.

If this was a learner in the classroom, what approach would you take if they were struggling with something? Do you work through the model to try and help them tackle the problem with a degree of independence? But you will cry, this is a colleague coming to you with a problem and you can do something to help! Instead of working down through the layers of the model, you have jumped straight to correcting. The very layer that should come last you are using first, you are doing the majority of the work, and the other person is perhaps doing very little, if any. They may well be grateful and appreciative but what is the learning that is taking place during this interaction? It might be worth considering how you can utilise the self-scaffolding model in your interactions in order to trigger reflection in your colleagues.

Your next steps

These final paragraphs are really an opportunity for you to consider where you currently are with your views, thoughts and confidence with coaching. Equally, another consideration is going to be where your school is with coaching practices. It is going to be a challenge using coaching techniques if the hierarchy are directive with their leadership.

If your school already has a coaching culture, then who can you work with that will help support your own coaching practices? If your school doesn't have a coaching culture, then which members of staff do you need to approach to put forward a case of adopting coaching techniques?

Reflection time

On average how many times during the working week do colleagues come to you to seek advice, including corridor conversations?

_____

_____

_____

_____

_____

_____

_____

How much time does this equate to during your working week and how does it impact on your own work?

_____
_____
_____
_____
_____
_____
_____

List the main reasons colleagues come to you for support, e.g. problems with a learner, behaviour, planning lessons, provision mapping, ideas for making reasonable adjustments, seeking a TA, etc.

_____
_____
_____
_____
_____
_____
_____

From the lists above, identify the reasons which staff return to you for advice on a regular basis.

_____
_____
_____
_____
_____
_____
_____

Identify what alternatives you could put in place to support staff other than having 1:1 'urgent' conversations.

Short-term solutions

_____
_____
_____
_____
_____
_____
_____

Long-term solutions

_____
_____
_____
_____
_____
_____

When you give advice, reflect on the following questions.

How much talking did I do?

_____
_____
_____
_____
_____
_____

How much listening did I do?

_____
_____
_____
_____
_____
_____

What did the other person do as a result of me giving advice?

_____

_____

_____

_____

_____

_____

_____

What actions will you take if you would like to further develop your coaching skills?

_____

_____

_____

_____

_____

_____

13 The whole you

The vision for you

We started this book with a chapter getting you to think about your vision for SEND. It is important to have a clear idea of what you want to work towards so that from time to time you can take a step back and see how you are progressing on your journey. Well, now we are focusing on the vision for *you*. You are always going to be a work in progress but how often do you stop to consider what you want to be in the future? We are not talking about job roles or status we are talking about the whole you!

This future you is an ambition for you to work towards. Perhaps it is a better, more effective leader who influences others and ensures inclusion is at the forefront of school developments. This person is going to enthuse and motivate others so that every individual across their setting takes responsibility for further developing and improving inclusive practices. This is no mean feat, but it is an opportunity to think big and plan for the future you: a great SENCo who listens, guides, supports and influences practices across their setting who has more sustainable approaches to managing their workload.

Current you

This is an opportunity to reflect on existing feelings or judgements you have about yourself across a range of areas. This is a reflection of the current you but is also an exercise to think about the vision of you in the future. We can all feel like we have areas for development and that at times we just aren't quite good enough but it's worth considering what the future you is going to look like and how you will lead successfully. This reflection might help you focus in more clearly on where you currently feel are currently performing in your role, with your practices and your behaviour.

To help with your reflections you may approach trusted colleagues who are willing to share their thoughts on particular areas of your role, leadership and behaviour. It may be you want to explore different areas that you want to better understand how you are performing in. It is entirely up to you what you focus on but it might be helpful to keep some focus on you as a SENCo and as a leader.

Approaching colleagues for their insight might be particularly useful if you are prone to being overly negative and critical of your own qualities and performance. Their insight might be able to provide a bit more balance. You may just have to remember that this is professional not personal, especially if you hear feedback which takes you by surprise or hadn't previously registered with you as perhaps being a negative trait.

A synopsis of reflections from each chapter

In many respects this chapter provides an opportunity to collate all your reflections from each chapter. What are you confident in and feel you are doing well at? What do you feel are areas that could be further developed to enhance how you lead SEND and inclusion across your setting? (And possibly beyond, if we are being ambitious here.)

Some questions to help start your reflections are:

- Which leadership styles do you currently use with confidence?
- How confident are you in influencing behaviours in your setting?
- How much do you understand about high-quality teaching?
- To what extent are you happy with how you respond to staff when they share concerns about SEND without having undertaken any reasonable adjustments to their practice?
- To what extent are you aware of the different types of assessments which can support the graduated approach in your setting?
- How do you currently feel about leading staff training?
- How do you feel you look and sound in front of your colleagues?
- How confident do you feel in speaking at meetings with different groups of stakeholders e.g. your own team meetings or with SLT?
- Do you know and understand enough about inclusion to undertake your role effectively?
- How confident do you feel about speaking up or challenging others when they are being negative about inclusive practices or inclusion on the whole?
- To what degree are you happy with your current work life balance?

What you can do is look at the previous chapters, read your reflections and use them to build the current you.

Questions to explore the future you:

- Which leadership styles do you want to use with more confidence in the future?
- What will your positive influencing behaviour look like in the future?
- What research can you draw on to help further your understanding of high-quality teaching?
- How do you want to look and feel when you are leading staff training?
- What aspects of inclusion would you like to know and understand in the future?
- Who will be in your network of support, who can help you, who can be trusted, who can challenge your thinking?
- What might a better work life balance involve in the future so you have time for family, friends, hobbies or leisure activities?

Both sets of questions are just starters to get you thinking. You are probably going to come up with much better questions to help focus your thinking and reflection.

Consider the future you

The idea is that once you have thought and reflected on the current you, you take time to think about the future you. This future you is going to be an impressive individual! Take some time to think about the behaviours, knowledge, understanding and awareness they will have. What is it about the future you that will lead with greater effectiveness whilst also ensuring that strategies and approaches are sustainable. Really consider what it is about the future you that will make a difference to inclusion in your setting. Think about the influence you will have, remember the leadership aspect is not about you working harder it is about you influencing the behaviour and actions of others more.

Let's walk through this activity together. It will be handy to have a piece of A3 paper with two columns and space at the bottom for you to record actions that will support your journey to the future you.

Current You	Future You
Behaviours How do I conduct myself around others, do I always present my 'best' self? Can I control my emotions when other challenge me? Do I give solutions before listening properly to what the actual issue is?	This is the ideal vision of you in the future. This is going to be whoever you feel is going to present the best version of you in a range of contexts. It is going to be a confident leader who listens to others, uses a variety of leadership styles to good effect.
Confidence Do I have the confidence to express myself clearly in meetings regardless of the audience? How do I feel about leading training sessions – small group or whole staff?	It might also be a future you where you achieve a better balance between dealing with operational challenges and focusing on strategic opportunities and developments.
Knowledge How much do I know about the different aspects of inclusion? how much do I know about high-quality teaching? Am I aware of different leadership styles? What do I currently know about change management?	The future you might also have more time for friends, family and hobbies so you achieve a better work life balance.
Leadership Which leadership styles do I generally default to? Are the leadership styles I use the most effective in different contexts?	
Awareness How aware am I of developments inside school within my local authority and nationally?	
Balance In an average week, how much time does work get and how much time do I get? Am I spending time doing the things that matter to me?	

Current You	Future You
Journey	
These are going to be the actions you are going to need to take in order for your future you to become more of a reality. What are you really going to commit to and engage with in order to be that better version of you?	

Journey from current to future you...

The journey is in some respects the actions you will need to take in order for you to make progress to the future you. You are not going to be this impressive individual overnight so you need to think about the different actions you can take that will support you on your journey. Some of these activities might be you working independently, some might be you taking advantage of the support networks and key staff around you.

A few ways to help you on your journey

Reading

This could be keeping up to date with the latest research or finding a theme that you might want to know more about. For instance, I am really interested in leadership and coaching so have read several books on the themes. This has helped me be 'luckier' in meetings and interactions by being able to draw on my learning and understanding from various books, which has then helped progress the situation I have found myself in.

Networking

You don't have to be an expert in every part of SEND but it helps to have contacts or colleagues that can shine a light on areas you aren't so familiar with. Networking also helps you avoid becoming institutionalised and gives you perspectives and insight into what works in other settings. These don't have to be face-to-face network meetings; there are several platforms you can use that will help you keep abreast of SEND and inclusion.

Shadowing

Go to see a SENCo or Inclusion Lead in their setting. What do they do in their setting? How do they address and deal with the challenges they face? What can you learn from this?

Training

This might just be training you need to undertake in order to do your job competently and effectively. It might be something as simple as getting a colleague to train you on how to effectively navigate your school management information system.

Professional development and learning

What can you focus on that will enhance how you lead as a SENCo or Inclusion Lead? It may be that you undertake a programme that helps you develop key skills and competencies over time, that make you more effective and impactful with the leadership aspect of your role. Unlike training, the professional development is going to help you grow as a professional and as a leader.

Listening

This might be something as simple as listening to colleagues in meetings so that you gain a wider perspective about what is happening in your setting. This listening might give you a greater awareness and understanding of what is happening across your school context. It might however be using travel time to listen to things like podcasts. Some of my best learning has come from listening into coaching podcasts whilst stuck in traffic or when I am out having a run.

Mentoring

This could be you becoming a mentor, which will help sharpen your own thinking about effective practice. Alternatively, it could be you identifying someone who can act as your mentor, someone who you respect and is able to share their knowledge, expertise and experience with humility.

Coaching

Same as the above -, you could become a coach, or you could select a coach. One reflection is that even if you work in a coaching school, it might be better for you to personally choose who you would work with rather than have a coach assigned to you. I say this because if the coach is your line manager and they are the issue (at that point in time) impacting on your work practices then that could derail the coaching interaction. Equally, if they are your line manager you may feel inhibited about sharing some of your areas for development for fear of how they may be used in future appraisals.

Reflection time

Giving yourself time to think and process what has happened in a day or over the course of a week. It may be that you keep a journal to record to your thoughts, how you acted, how others reacted and the outcome of the situation. Allowing yourself time to reflect allows learning opportunities but also provides an opportunity to park an irritating issue and put it into context.

Challenges

This could be something that takes you outside your comfort zone but in doing so provides you with a development opportunity. One of my biggest challenges I took on as a new SENCo was leading a whole staff training session. More than 100 staff in a hall with me talking about new approaches to SEND in our setting. It caused me some sleepless nights in the lead up, but it helped to shine a light on what I did well and what I needed to be better at. What challenge will you take that pushes you out of your comfort zone but will help you get better in your role?

Hobbies and Interests

Following on from the time management exercise, what doesn't feel urgent but is extremely important is having time for you. It may be that you need a distraction from work, something to take your mind off emails, paperwork or meetings. Perhaps that means finding an interest or a hobby which provides the outlet for you to regain some balance in your life. For me I have running but I also have cooking (more specifically Spanish cooking to experiment with new dishes and tapas for my family). The cooking provides a focus, and time takes on a different dimension when I'm doing it, so I find it quite therapeutic.

It is down to you to think about what is going to be essential to help you on your journey. Again, the above ideas are a starter. Based on you and your context you might come up with different ideas that will be equally as effective and helpful in supporting your ongoing progress and development.

Conclusion

Good luck with your continued journey…

I'll keep this short to conclude. Being a great leader is not a destination, it is an evolving process where you continue to learn, adapt and evolve your practices and approaches. I hope that this book has been helpful in shining a light on possible areas that will support you on your journey. You are going to make mistakes along the way, but you aren't making them on purpose so don't beat yourself up. See each mistake as a learning opportunity and try to avoid making the same mistakes over and over.

Good luck with your continued journey. I hope you find enjoyment and challenge in equal measures with your current and future roles.